Other books by Claudine Burnett:

Died in Long Beach: Cemetery Tales.

Fighting Fear: Long Beach in the 1940s.

From Barley Fields to Oil Town: a Tour of Huntington Beach, 1901-1922.

Haunted Long Beach.

Haunted Long Beach 2.

Murderous intent? Long Beach, CA. 1880's-1920.

Prohibition Madness.

Soaring Skyward: A History of Aviation in and around Long Beach, CA.

Strange Sea Tales Along the Southern California Coast.

Jointly with other authors:

Surfing Newport Beach: the Glory Days of Corona del Mar. With Paul Burnett.

The Heritage of African Americans in Long Beach.
In association with the African American Heritage Society of Long Beach, Aaron L. Day and Indira Hale Tucker.

Balboa Films: a history and filmography of the silent film studio. With Jean-Jacques Jura and Rodney Norman Bardin II.

The Red Scare, UFOs & Elvis:

Long Beach Enters the Atomic Age

Claudine Burnett

authorHOUSE®

AuthorHouse™
1663 Liberty Drive
Bloomington, IN 47403
www.authorhouse.com
Phone: 1 (800) 839-8640

Published by AuthorHouse 06/29/2018

ISBN: 978-1-5462-4723-4 (sc)
ISBN: 978-1-5462-4722-7 (e)

Library of Congress Control Number: 2018907068

Print information available on the last page.

This book is printed on acid-free paper.

Dedicated to Baby Boomers
Who Remember
And
Others Who Want to Learn

Table of Contents

Introduction

Imagine waking up to the sound of a civil defense siren blaring from your cell phone. You go to the phone and read the message:

Emergency Alert
BALLISTIC MISSILE THREAT INBOUND TO HAWAII.
SEEK IMMEDIATE SHELTER. THIS IS NOT A DRILL.

Such was the case with me and thousands of others at 8:07 a.m. on Saturday, January 13, 2018. For some it was panic, a dash to a protective bathtub. For others, a resigned acceptance, thinking that staring at the beauty of Hawaii was not a bad way to go. For me I recalled the chapter I had written in this book about what to do in such an attack:

- *First indication of an atomic burst will be a sudden burst of light. If possible, don't look at the light. Try to cover all exposed parts of the body.*
- *If you are in the open when the sudden light comes, drop instantly to the ground and curl up to cover bare arms and hands, neck and face with clothing. The curled-up position should be held for at least 10 seconds with your back to the light before standing up.*
- *If you are in the street and some sort of protection such as a doorway, a corner, or a tree is no more than a step or two*

away, you may take shelter there with your back to the light and in a crouched position.

- *Wait at least 10 seconds before you stand up. No attempt should be made to reach a shelter if it is several steps off.*

I also recollected the grim fact that if you were within 15 miles of the impact point your probability of survival was pretty slim. The further away you were your chances of coming out alive were much improved. I realized that Honolulu was probably the initial target. I thought it an amazing coincidence that World War III might also be triggered by an attack on Oahu, just like what had happened in World War II. I was on Kauai; 110 miles from the beaches of Waikiki, far from what I thought might be the designated target. But then I remembered the U.S. missile base on Kauai. It was about 30 miles from where I was staying. Could that be the foreign missile's objective? To destroy U.S. missiles and keep the U.S. from having a quick means to retaliate?

I recalled what Truman Bethurum told a Long Beach audience in September 1954, that there would never be an atomic war "because people from outer space will see to that." He went on to say the aliens had the power to nullify the bombs and would do so if it became necessary. Well, I hoped he was right!

As these thoughts passed through my mind I sent out an e-mail telling folks that I loved them no matter what happened. After sending the e-mail I looked at news reports online. Eighteen minutes after the initial alert, it was corrected; but there was no follow-up mobile text for 38 minutes. It seemed an employee at Hawaii's Emergency Management Agency had actually thought a real attack was eminent. He hadn't gotten the message that it was just a drill.

I grew up in the 50s and 60s–the beginnings of the atomic age. When I began working for the City of Long Beach in 1971 I immediately became a civil defense worker. City employees were given training in an underground bunker at the Municipal Airport and told what role they would play in case of an attack. Chances were that Long Beach with its navy base, Douglas Aircraft, and nearby Seal Beach Naval Weapons Station would be a prime target. We were prepared! But as the 70s ebbed into the 80s, the yearly civil defense training became less intense and finally ended as did the bunker at the airport. The Cold War was over. No longer did new city employees have to take civil defense training or sign a loyalty oath to the United States as I had.

As I write this book I am finding that history is indeed repeating itself. The threat of a nuclear war again has folks in a panic. Will it come from Russia, North Korea, Iran or elsewhere? Will "duck and cover" drills, such as I experienced growing up, again become standard practice in schools? Will peace talks finally succeed in officially ending a war in Korea that has been going on for almost 70 years, and will North Korea stick to their pledge to give up nuclear weapons? What of Russia and Iran? Need we fear their nuclear capabilities?

I hope that by reading this book you will uncover an interesting period in Southern California history. America had entered the atomic age. Flying saucers were big news, Communism appeared rampant, a war in Korea erupted, teens turned to murder, and there was fear the world might end. It was also a time of transition. Rock 'n' roll entered the scene, space flight became a reality, and the public learned not to blindly accept what the government told them, especially when it came to atomic radiation and waste.

UFOs

The wave of UFO sightings that began in 1947 seemed strange, mysterious and often unnerving to Long Beach residents. However, if they would have looked further back into the city's history they would have discovered earlier appearances of unidentified objects. Captain Billie Graves reported seeing "strange phenomena" in the sky in July 1907. In October 1911, spectators along the city's waterfront were astonished to see four huge structures, looking like floating towers, approaching from the direction of Catalina Island. The huge objects advanced more closely and the wind caused the light mist to disappear. Some said it was a mirage brought on by peculiar atmospheric conditions in the Catalina channel, others weren't so sure, having experienced a strange feeling as though something strange was due to happen.

Nothing more strange than the phenomena itself happened that October day, but five years later something did - frogs dropping from the sky! On October 2, 1916, thousands of small frogs, which apparently came with a storm, littered the ground on Seaside Boulevard. No one could identify what kind of frogs they were, but their concert of croaks and their odor kept many residents awake throughout the night.

These were isolated events, easily explained as "natural phenomena," but the sightings of unidentified objects which began in 1947 continue unabated up to the present day. Let's look at what Long Beach residents claimed they saw.

On the evening of January 6, 1947, observers in Long Beach saw a strange weirdly flashing object plunge towards the sea. Sighted all the way from Bakersfield to San Diego, authorities assured callers it was an exceptionally large meteor. But was it really? Could it have been the prelude to a rash of UFO sightings that came to haunt the skies of the nation June through August 1947?

On July 4, 1947, hundreds of people throughout the west saw mysterious sky disks that zipped above them in the Independence Day sky. Were they the same ones that had first appeared on June 24 over Washington State? Nearly all the observers agreed that the objects, whatever they were, were round, flat and shiny.

W.G. Ebermayer of 3924 ½ E. 14th Street in Long Beach claimed he saw one of the flying discs about 1:22 a.m. on the morning of the 4th. As he was walking home from his parked car near Mira Mar Avenue and Fountain Street he saw the weird object over Lakewood Village. He was sure it was not a meteor because as it came closer he observed a brilliant red object, with ragged edges and an irregular shape. As it approached the ground it dipped near the surface and disappeared.

A few days earlier H.D. Anderson, 138 Glendora Avenue, reported seeing a "fiery object" just before dusk heading south. He said it was not a jet and seemed to drop into the ocean. Danny Carroll, 284 East 56th Street, and a half dozen people in his neighborhood saw two flaming objects in the sky after dark on July 5th. These UFOs were also going southward.

Kenneth Arnold, who started the flying saucer craze when he reported seeing "rocketing saucers" on June 24, 1947, while he was flying over the Pacific Northwest, said the strange objects shooting through the air at great speeds could not be airplanes. He claimed they were at least as large as or larger than an airplane and apparently meant no harm.

Government officials had rational explanations for the mysterious sightings. Skeptical scientists recalled the mysterious "rockets" seen over Sweden in 1946. Eighty percent of these "ghost rockets" proved to be meteors, and Swedish officials said the other 30 percent could be discounted as pure imagination.

Scientists, such as Dr. Gerhard Kuiper director of the Yerkes Observatory in Williams Bay, Wisconsin, believed the flying discs were not meteors. Dr. Kuiper thought the saucers were being controlled either by our armed services or were sent here from abroad. An unidentified Manhattan Project scientist, according to the July 6, 1947 *Independent*, reportedly said the discs were being used in connection with experiments in "transmutation of atomic energy." He claimed experiments were being conducted at Muroc Lake in Southern California, at White Sands in New Mexico, at Portland, Oregon, and in other places. The scientist declared: "These 'saucers' so-called, are capable of high speeds but they can be controlled from the ground. They are 20 feet in width in the center and are partially rocket-propelled on the take-off." He said people were not 'seeing things.' The flying discs were a government experiment and any further information on the discs would have to come from the war department. However, the government claimed no knowledge of this experiment.

Imagination or not, bathers in the Belmont Shore area of Long Beach reported three objects resembling silvery balloons flying in a triangular formation on the afternoon of July 8, 1947. Virginia Lamb, 340 Oregon Avenue, and a group of 12 teenagers saw three saucer shaped discs over the beach at the foot of Coronado Avenue around 2:30 p.m. Mrs. Lamb reported the saucers had rims that were "too high to have been visible if they were merely balloons." She said they flew in a triangular formation and the triangle revolved in a "dancing manner." They were traveling east and disappeared shortly after they were sighted. One bather who only caught a glimpse of one object said it blew up in a puff of smoke as he was watching it.

Mrs. Helen Ruttgen, 6025 Falcon, Long Beach, reported that on the night of July 8th she and her husband saw one of the flying objects while they were taking a walk. She told authorities the UFO was fiery and appeared to have sparks coming from it. Mrs. Ruttgen said they observed the object for five minutes and that it had a slight reddish color. It appeared to be about the size of a large star. The object was spotted about 9:10 p.m. and, according to Mrs. Ruttgen, would speed along, then slow down and then go fast again.

Mrs. Beulah Hudson of 380 Mira Mar Avenue, Long Beach, also reported seeing a flying disc that same evening while walking her dog near her home. The disc, silvery and round, was speeding north by east, she said, and was directly overhead when she first saw it.

Interestingly, July 8, 1947, also coincided with the date the military issued a press release stating the 509th Bomb Group had recovered a "flying disc," which had crashed on a ranch near Roswell, New Mexico. The *San Francisco Chronicle* printed the following:

The many rumors regarding the flying disc became a reality yesterday when the intelligence office of the 509th Bomb Group of the Eighth Air Force, Roswell Army Air Field, was fortunate enough to gain possession of a disc through the cooperation of one of the local ranchers and the Sheriff's Office of Chaves County.

The flying object landed on a ranch near Roswell sometime last week. Not having phone facilities, the rancher stored the disc until such time as he was able to contact the Sherriff's office, who in turn notified Major Jesse A. Marcel, of the 509th Bomb Group Intelligence Office.

Action was immediately taken and the disc was picked up at the rancher's home. It was inspected at the Roswell Army Air Field and subsequently loaned by Major Marcel to higher headquarters.

Three hours after Army press officer Walter Haut dropped off the report to KGFL radio station in Roswell, and picked up by the news media, the Army changed its mind about the report. Haut was sent back to KGFL with a second press release stating that the first press release had been incorrect. The debris was nothing more than a weather balloon. It was too late for some newspapers, such as the *San Francisco Chronicle,* to retract the original story.

What is known is that the object appeared in the middle of a powerful lightning storm before crashing on W.W. Brazel's ranch.

Brazel first found the remnants on June 14, 1947, and put the pieces into his pickup truck and drove them to the local sheriff's office in Roswell. Following the second press release, the story faded. No one in the town of Roswell spoke of it publicly for more than thirty years. Then in 1978 Stan Friedman showed up in Roswell and began asking questions. After two years of research, Friedman and his research partner Bill Moore had interviewed more than sixty-two original witnesses to the Roswell incident.

It appeared that a lot more had happened in Roswell in the first and second weeks of July 1947 than just a weather balloon crash. The first hint that something was amiss was when a large number of military descended upon the town. Brazel, who found the remnants, was jailed for almost a week. Some witnesses saw military police loading large boxes and crates onto military trucks and aircraft. The local coroner received a mysterious call requesting several child-size coffins that could be hermetically sealed. Townsfolk were threatened with federal prison time if they spoke about what they saw. Friedman and Moore found the stories relayed by the sixty-two witnesses had two factors in common. The first was that the crash involved a flying saucer, or round disc. The second assertion was amazing. Witnesses said they saw bodies. Not just any old bodies but child-size, humanoid-type beings with large heads, big oval eyes, and no noses, that had apparently been inside the flying saucer. In 1980, Friedman and Moore published a book called *The Roswell Incident* and Roswell became the pinnacle of UFO events.

Were the UFO sightings which occurred before and after the Roswell crash in 1947, somehow related? In Long Beach, after a number of "discless" days, Paul R. Rioth (1331 Junipero Avenue) phoned in a new report to the *Press-Telegram*. Rioth said he and his wife were in their backyard with friends watching a skywriter at 6:05 p.m. on July 25th. Then a round object came into view four seconds before it raced across the sky. The body appeared to be about 6 feet in diameter, traveling northwest at an altitude of about 1800 feet. Trailing behind the disc was a path of smoke with a reddish flame. In the four seconds the object was visible it traveled a mile, Rioth said; he estimated its speed to be 900 miles an hour. He told skeptical reporters his claim of seeing this strange vehicle was definitely not a hoax.

After reading the article in the *Press-Telegram* others came forward with similar tales. Mr. And Mrs. Harry Kessler (3477 Orange), John Salerno (1528 Linden), and four persons at the W.J.K. Walker home (2603 E. Pacific Coast Highway), added their testimonies to the Rioth story about the flying saucer. All claimed they saw the same object at the same time. Mrs. Walker added a further bit of information saying that before the speeding disc disappeared she saw three or four pieces, which she called little discs, break away from it. Could it have been an aircraft transport releasing smaller aircraft, as officials later claimed?

Flying saucers seemed to generally avoid the Long Beach skies through much of 1948 and 1949, though a few sightings were reported. On February 6, 1948, a "squadron" of 15 silver discs was seen spinning at lightning speed over the oil derricks of Signal Hill. Witnesses at 4552 Lime Avenue described them as being about the size of a small plane, but with an internal glow. The observers watched as the flickering saucers moved from formation and then back into a pattern. Seconds later they disappeared in the direction of the ocean.

On March 7, 1948, mysterious lights were observed in the sky, but these were explained away as being a meteor. In May 1949, Mrs. Marie Ofield saw a flock of birds outside her window. When the birds flew out of view she caught sight of a circular black object which seemed to be floating in the air several blocks away and a few hundred feet in the air. She called others to watch as the object, which appeared to be the size and shape of a saucer, drift out of sight.

On June 2, 1949, Ruth Jussila was sunbathing in her daughter's yard at 4318 Pepperwood when she saw a "flying disc" about 1:20 p.m. She had been watching an airplane cross the sky, but about two minutes after it passed from view the disc came along, in a straight line. Gradually it faded away as though it was going higher. Mrs.

Jussila, who said she used to scoff at such stories as flying saucers, was now a believer.

In October 1949, pilots spotted an object looking like a flying saucer, but it was later found to be a weather balloon sent up by the Long Beach Army Air Force base for transmitting weather and wind data. Normally the balloons burst about 50,000 feet, but this one climbed to 70,000 feet before it exploded, causing pilots to question its nature.

In April 1949, Washington, D.C., placed "secrecy restrictions" on certain incidents connected with flying saucers. Earlier that year radio reporter Walter Winchell claimed the saucers came from Russia. The United States government didn't deny Winchell's assertion, saying it was impossible to "deny categorically" that the weird objects originated in the Soviet Union or any other nation, and that indeed there were "inexplicable" incidents placed in the "classified" category, denied to all persons except authorized military personnel.

The mysterious unidentified flying objects again made a Long Beach appearance in 1950, shortly after the Russians exploded their first atomic bomb on August 29, 1949. In March 1950 two Long Beach Air Force sergeants and 100 other individuals reported a metallic saucer-like object in the skies at the mountain resort of Idyllwild. Sergeants Robert O'Hara and Sherwood Elder were using field glasses to watch exhaust trails from a jet aircraft when they noticed a strange disc flying at around 30,000 feet. Although the vapor trails were blown in a southwesterly direction, the disc moved steadily northward for four hours before disappearing over the mountains.

Most sightings were imaginary, Air Force officials claimed, or simply weather balloons as the one sighted near Long Beach's Douglas Aircraft Company on August 8, 1950. All could be explained rationally, the military said. They were not part of an invasion force from outer space or some other country as some claimed.

Mary Mikkelson wasn't so sure about the government's explanation after she saw "a half-moon shaped object surrounded by small lights zooming low in the sky" while sitting on her back porch at 1324 Pine Avenue in March 1950, which suddenly disappeared. Nor did the V.M. Hill family who reported seeing a shiny, circular object that seemed to pause in flight over Long Beach and then suddenly "take off and disappear to the east very fast."

On July 23, 1952, almost 100 sky watchers throughout Long Beach reported seeing a flying saucer at dusk. In Washington, D.C, an Air Force spokesman denied emphatically that the Air Force had put volunteer aircraft spotters on 24-hour duty because of a possible flying saucer invasion. They claimed the reason for the spotters was to supplement the radar network by watching for unidentified low-flying aircraft from other nations. Whatever the reason for calling the aircraft spotters out in force, an unidentified object, sparkling in the setting sun, was first seen by more than a dozen North Long Beach residents around 7:30 p.m. This initial report was followed by scores of others in the area. All agreed the object floated "lazily" over the Long Beach area at first, but later picked up speed and headed northwest. As it sped away the object split in two and the two segments disappeared, moving in different directions at a tremendous speed. This was the fourth such sighting in a week. The platter shaped objects had all appeared between 7 and 8 p.m. each time in approximately the same area, high in the sky. The Long Beach Air Force Weather Station, at the Municipal Airport, assured the public they were simply weather balloons. The balloons often climbed as high as 10 miles over Long Beach and while they gained altitude they often picked up air and ice. This ice could shine brilliantly in the sun.

On January 28, 1953, fiery, disc-like objects were sighted over Southern California. At times they appeared motionless, other times they outraced pursuing jet aircraft. They were first spotted after military pilots flying at 20,000 feet near Corona reported a terrific explosion high above them at 7:55 p.m. Jet pilots from the El Toro Marine Base that had reported the blast were told to investigate, but they were unable to catch whatever it was. One object, which was moving at various elevations and was amber in color, was estimated to have been traveling over 500 m.p.h. An 11 year Marine Air Corps pilot reported they were able to trail it as far as Long Beach.

The Long Beach Airport control tower logged a similar object spewing orange flames and tracked it until it disappeared six minutes later out to sea. The official log read:

At 9 p.m. there appeared an eerie orange flame such as the furtive playing of a powerful searchlight beam. This was seen several times in two minutes at a height of 100 feet. At 9:03 p.m. the object was directly west of the airport at 2000 feet and was westbound. At 9:06 p.m. the object disappeared into the west. (Press-Telegram 1/29/1953)

The following day Navy fliers observed four discs flying in formation over Malibu. They were described as being about the size of a B-36 aircraft, but circular, of aluminum color and flying in formation. "They definitely were not balloons or any type of aircraft I have ever seen," pilot Jay Mattis told the *Press-Telegram*. "I'm a confirmed believer now in the saucers or whatever you want to call them. If they had been balloons they wouldn't have been moving so fast. Their speed was terrific. They traveled 100 miles in about five minutes."

Not everyone had a rational explanation for the unidentified flying objects buzzing the skies. There were those who believed they came from further afield, perhaps Russia or even the stars. Some reports were definitely bogus, such as the one on February 19, 1953, when a man removed his trousers and sat down at the counter of a Long Beach Boulevard café. "I've just seen 75 men from Mars," he announced. "You'd better get out of here." When police came, he asked "Are you from Mars." They said yes. Satisfied, he went to jail.

On October 4, 1957, fear and awe gripped the American public—the Soviets had launched a satellite into orbit around the earth. Could the Russians now launch a nuclear attack on the U.S. from outer space? The satellite traveled 560 miles above the earth, circling the globe every 96.2 minutes. Its orbit brought it over the United States seven times every 24 hours. Two American scientists said the Soviet launched sphere was sending back coded messages they were unable to decipher. The craft was also hard to spot. Scientists were sure the Russians had chosen to launch the satellite at such an angle to the sun as to prevent visual observations in the free world. How long would it continue to whirl through the heavens? Estimates ranged from a few days to a million years.

American researchers had been working on a U.S. satellite for a number of years. They hoped to launch the 21.5 pound satellite sometimes in 1958, but the Russians had beaten them; not only was the Soviet Union the first nation on this planet to get to outer space, but their satellite weighed an awesome 184 pounds. To launch such a satellite took a tremendous rocket, something the Americans refused to admit they didn't have. Some government officials said the launching of the Russian satellite proved beyond a shadow of a doubt that the Soviets had the "ultimate weapon" – a long range missile capable of delivering atomic and hydrogen explosives across continents and oceans. Many worried about the future of the United States since there had just been a cut in funding the Defense Department's missile program.

There was some cause for hope. In November 1957, Douglas Aircraft officials leaked news of a secret study they were conducting to learn how men would react to space flight. The unnamed source indicated the research had been going on in Long Beach for two years. Also, news arrived in December that construction had started on the nation's first nuclear-powered missile cruiser, the USS Long Beach. Surely, it would be able to protect us from the Russians.

A month after the Soviet launching, the skies of Southern California became cluttered with unidentified flying objects. Three Air Force weather observers and 10 military personnel awaiting a flight at Long Beach Municipal Airport observed six saucer-shaped or spherical UFOs at the base of 7000-foot clouds over the airport at 3:50 p.m. on November 5, 1957. Los Alamitos Naval Air Station personnel said they saw UFOs almost continuously between 6:05 and 7:25 p.m. the same day.

The airmen claimed they saw the unidentied objects darting in and out of the clouds at the base of the cumulonimbus. The objects appeared to be circular in shape and shiny like spun aluminum. They also seemed to have the ability to change course instantaneously with no loss of speed. Based on their knowledge of aircraft, the pilots thought the objects were larger than a C-46, a two-engine Air Force transport plane. After discussing possible rational explanations for the phenomena, they rejected the theory that the objects were sheet ice from the cloud pack because of the regular, circular shape of the six "things." The airmen also knew they were not balloons.

Police in the Los Angeles-Long Beach area received more than 100 phone calls about the UFOs and mysterious lights that November evening. Hollywood Hills residents reported a "ball of fire" in the sky. San Fernando Valley residents said they saw a "great green light" visible for less than a minute before it disappeared.

U.S. Weather Bureau officials reported no atmospheric conditions which could account for the reports. Dr. Dinsmore Alter, head of the Griffith Park Observatory, said "unsteady air" had caused the planet Venus to shine brighter than normal. And, he said, the star Arcturus in the northeast was sparkling brighter than usual. Lockheed Air Terminal tower employees in Burbank said the light seen by Hollywood and Valley residents may have been a falling star reported about 7:30 p.m. Whatever it was, many people saw it.

Following the November 5th sightings, Long Beach resident Edward Ruppelt, former head of the Air Force's *Project Blue Book* investigating unidentified flying objects, stated the government needed to step up its probe of UFO sightings. Ruppelt, head of Project Blue Book from 1951 to 1953, said seven top scientists urged more money for an intensified investigation in 1953. He said the scientists decided the evidence did not then justify the conclusion that the flying objects were visitors from outer space, but they did recommend intensified investigation. However, several military advisors, Ruppelt recalled, firmly believed the objects were from alien worlds.

Ruppelt, now an aircraft research engineer specializing in weapons systems, said he was intrigued and fascinated by reports of missile engineers and others in southwestern states who reported automobile motors stopping and lights dimming when approached by mysterious, glowing, egg-shaped objects. Air Force officials, however, claimed that 98 percent of past UFO reports could be explained by natural phenomena.

Edward Ruppelt also had a tale to tell; and tell it he did in a book he authored entitled *The Report on Unidentified Flying Objects.* In the book Ruppelt was the first to use the term "unidentified flying object," to replace the terms "flying saucer" and "flying disc," which he felt were misleading when applied to unknown objects of different shapes. The book, published in 1956, was also the first to be written by a member of Project Blue Book, the official Air Force investigation committee. Astronomer and Blue Book consultant J. Allen Hynek suggested that Ruppelt's book should be required reading for anyone seriously interested in UFOs.

Ruppelt had gotten hold of several "suppressed" stories about the Air Force's involvement with UFOs, which he discussed in detail. One told of a jet pilot who had been sent up to investigate a UFO. The pilot followed the saucer for two minutes, drawing within 500 yards of it. Suddenly it began to pull away from his jet, and the pilot immediately made up his mind to stop it – he began to shoot. Needless to say the bullets didn't stop the mystery object and the pilot's squadron commander ordered the report of the incident destroyed because he felt the pilot had "cracked up."

Ruppelt related scores of other saucer incidents he had investigated during his two years heading Project Blue Book. For many he had rational explanations, but in dozens of cases his investigators came up with no reasonable explanation for saucer sightings. In the "unknown" category was a 1951 incident over Long Beach in which a group of F-86 jets tried to approach a silvery object circling 11 miles up in the sky. The F-86s couldn't reach it, and in 1951 nothing the U.S. government had could fly higher than an F-86. Ed Ruppelt said even after his involvement in Project Blue Book he was still as baffled as when he began because there was no aircraft on this earth which could so handily out distance our latest jets.

Frustrated because of funding cuts and bureaucratic entanglements involved in Project Blue Book, Ruppelt retired from the Air Force and went to work as a research engineer for Northrop Aircraft Company.

Interestingly, after Ruppelt resigned from the project a joint military regulation was passed making it a crime for military personnel to discuss classified UFO reports with unauthorized persons. Violators faced up to 2 years in prison and/or fines of up to $10,000.

Edward Ruppelt continued to live in Long Beach until his death of a heart attack on September 15, 1960. He was 37 years old.

Throughout America UFO clubs were formed to study the unexplained phenomena. Some were serious researchers, others a bit nutty. In Long Beach, two groups were founded by Long Beach UFO enthusiasts in the 1950s – the UFO Research Society (it later changed its name to the Cosmic Research Society and the Long Beach Interplanetary Research Group (which later became "Interplanetary Research Group: Understanding Unit No. 8," an American and Canadian organization "devoted to better understanding among the peoples of earth and bringing understanding between the people of this earth and those of other planets) to discuss the phenomena. The UFO Research Society was led by Reverend Carl Anderson, who claimed to have been contacted by beings from outer space. The Interplanetary Research Group wasn't sure about Anderson and his claims, and they wanted to distance themselves from his preconceived notions about UFOs – they considered themselves open-minded and were anxious to hear all points of view.

One of the Interplanetary Research Group's first speakers was Truman Bethurum, a former Long Beach resident, who addressed a skeptical audience in September 1954. He told how space men led him into their 300-foot flying saucer not just once, but eleven times!

The crew appeared human, and was headed by a female captain, Aura Rhanes. All spoke colloquial English, Bethurum claimed, and came from the planet Clarion on the other side of our moon, which could not be seen from earth. Bethurum revealed they took him on trips across country and were here to end war without killing anyone. Bethurum, the author of *Aboard a Flying Saucer,* revealed that President Eisenhower had also talked with one of these space men.

Bethurum apologized for lack of photographic evidence, saying he had made photographs of the disc on two occasions, but all he got were reflections of metal. He did, however, show an artist's conception of the 300-foot disc he said came from Clarion, the mysterious planet beyond the moon. Bethurum did have some reassuring news. He told the audience of 250 that he believed there would never be an atomic war "because people from outer space will see to that." He went on to say the aliens had the power to nullify the bombs and would do so if it became necessary. Mankind would never gain the secrets of flying saucer power, Bethurum added, until humankind lost the desire to fight each other. Bethurum achieved a bit of notoriety after his story came out. He even started a religious commune near Prescott, Arizona, after the space aliens told him to do so.

Another speaker was Calvin C. Girvin who addressed the UFO Research Society in September 1956.

Girvin had an interesting story to tell, claiming to have spotted about 75 flying saucers in the past eight years. He said his first encounter was in November 1954 when he was stationed at Hickham Field, Hawaii. He was just about to go to bed when he saw a blue-white light streaking through the night sky, leaving a trail of red sparks. Figuring it was a just a jet the sergeant fell asleep. What happened then could have been a dream, he admitted, but it was like no dream he had ever had. He felt himself leave the house and over the yard, about three feet above the ground, was a ball shaped object approximately 35 feet in diameter. Its pearl-like cover glowed blue. A voice told him to enter the craft; after he did so he was whisked to another bigger violet colored space ship.

Taken to a UFO conference room, he saw 30 or 40 earth looking creatures dressed in earth style clothing; they identified themselves as being from outer space. They chatted amiably for about 45 minutes about Girvin's future before he was transported back to his room at Hickham Field. When he woke up the next morning he was already dressed. Not only that – a circle 35 feet in diameter was burned into the lawn.

Girvin later described his encounters in a book *The Night Has a Thousand Saucers* published in 1958. It differed greatly from what he told the UFO Research Society in 1956.

In the book Girvin said he became interested in flying saucers after reading about UFO sightings in 1947. He soon began to have dreams, and joined the Air Force because he was told to do so by his Venusian friends, Cryxtan and Ashtar, to act as their spy. They wanted him to use every opportunity to inspect any files, reports, photographs or other evidence the Air Force held on flying saucers. At first he only remembered his encounters through dreams, but on September 15, 1952, while driving to Washington, D.C., he saw a Venusian saucer land and got to ride up to the alien mother ship which was orbiting the earth. He did what the aliens asked him and joined the Air Force. He was delighted when he was assigned to the Pentagon, even if it was only in food services, and used every opportunity to strike up conversations about saucers with top military officials. After a few months, Pentagon officials, tired of his incessant banter about UFOs, transferred him to Hawaii.

Long Beach's Reverend Carl Anderson, president of the UFO Research Society was a believer. He was also a minister of the Universal Church of the Master, chartered in 1918, which dealt in "metaphysics, the study of psychic phenomena and modern thinking." When not investigating UFOs he worked as an acoustic tile installer to make financial ends meet. He and his family had three encounters with flying saucers, he told members of the group he founded.

All three times Anderson was camped on the Mojave Desert; during one of the visitations the badly burned hand of a friend was cured by a greenish light emanating from a huge hovering spaceship. The first encounter was in April 1954, when the Anderson's were paralyzed by a beam of light coming from a flying saucer that had landed. Anderson wrote a book, *Two Nights to Remember*, about his experiences, which came out shortly after his taped communication with Mon-Ka of Mars.

In 1956, Anderson had all of Southern California astir with his claim that on November 7, 1956, a momentous event was going to occur. On that day, Mon-Ka, head of the Martian Space Confederation would speak to the people of earth on television and radio.

Mon-Ka's message about his visit came via a tape recorder to members of the Long Beach UFO Research Society in September 1956. The slow-speaking Martian told members that his craft would hover over Los Angeles at an altitude of 10,000 feet; he would then deliver a two-minute message of good will which he would broadcast on television and radio. He asked the Society to request that no military force be used to stop him, or it would prove disastrous to the American aircraft.

Mon-Ka, recording from station KOR on Mars, described life on his planet. He told the research group that science and art was far in advance of Earth's and that citizens enjoyed a 400-year lifespan by periodic visits to a "revitalizing chamber." Workers on the red planet only labored four hours a day, spending the balance in study, recreation and leisure. Manufacturing was accomplished by thought-controlled automation machines. One of these industries produced 45 percent of the Space Confederation's space ships.

There were several tape recordings from Mon-Ka heard by the group, which met regularly to correlate evidences of planetary visitations. All the communications Reverend Anderson had gathered were in English, but Anderson said the men from space usually spoke very slowly.

UFO enthusiasts waited with eager anticipation for Mon-Ka to beam his message. Television channel 13 even provided live coverage. Mon-Ka didn't make it. "There could have been some confusion as to dates," admitted Reverend Anderson. "There's still a possibility Mon-Ka may make his appearance in the next few days." Anderson was pleased to announce, however, that ten harbor area residents spotted strange lights in the sky about the time Mon-Ka was supposed to be hovering over the area in his flying saucer. Maybe the Martian just had a communications problem. Truman Bethurum had an answer. He claimed people from outer space just weren't interested in proving anything to anyone. He should know, he said, he'd had numerous contacts with "tourists" from the planet Clarion who communicated with him telepathically.

Former Air Force staff sergeant Calvin Girvin said he was in contact with another interplanetary plenipotentiary, Ashtar of Venus. Ashtar told him government restrictions made an interstellar tete-a-tete impossible. Could that have been the reason Mon-Ka hadn't been able to appear? The rival Long Beach UFO organization, the Interplanetary Research Group, thought it was all a ploy to sell Anderson's forthcoming book.

What of Anderson and Mon-Ka? By 1960, Mon-Ka had been replaced by another alien named Kumar who explained the spaceship's propulsion system to Anderson. Kumar instructed Anderson to travel to Germany and meet with German engineers, including rocket scientist Hermann Oberth, and share the information with him. This he did, and the two met for three days. Kumar, who claimed he was from Mars, visited Anderson several times. Anderson was impressed that Kumar often levitated and performed other remarkable feats, including suddenly vanishing into thin air. According to author Paul Christopher, Kumar last contacted Anderson in the Mojave Desert the night of May 4, 1963.

In April 1957 the Anderson led UFO Research Society invited Hope Troxell to speak. Troxell claimed to have made contact with space ships from alien planets which she wrote about in her book *Wisdom from Outer Space*. Troxell, a Pasadena interior decorator and adult education teacher at Glendale College, believed she had received three major healings from "angelic hosts" in her early life. During the 1950s she obtained instructions from these "masters" which she wrote about in her book. Were these "masters" aliens from outer space? In later years Troxell received a vision that Carson Peak near June Lake, California, was a major UFO pathway. Following her vision she moved to June Lake and in 1963 started the Church of the Cosmic Origin.

April 1957 was a busy month for local UFO enthusiasts. That same month the Interplanetary Research Group organization hosted George W. Van Tassel, owner and operator of the Giant Rock Airport where airplanes and other strange craft such as UFOs were said to land. According to Van Tassel, the aliens were interdimensional beings that normally couldn't be seen, but you could talk to them in English. Van Tassel had set aside 10 acres at his landing site between Victorville and Yucca Valley to study the mysteries of rejuvenation which the aliens revealed to him. Here he built what he called an "Integraton" which would recharge and rejuvenate people's cells. The Integraton was never fully completed because of Van Tassel's death from a heart attack in 1978. However, the Integraton is still at Giant Rock, and some claim to be rejuvenated just by being near it.

Most members of the Interplanetary Research Group, such as chiropractor Dr. E.O. Hendricks, had joined the organization to gather all the information they could about interplanetary subjects to help them make a rational decision about the validity of alien visitors. Others were already convinced the aliens were real and looked upon the possible arrival of aliens from outer space with much anticipation. One of them was a pleasant white-haired woman named Mary Thomas, secretary of the group.

In December 1957, Mary Thomas stood in the back of the YWCA auditorium in Long Beach waiting for the meeting of the Interplanetary Research Group to come to order. Most of the 32 people in the audience came into the auditorium in all seriousness; however reporter Bob Whearley didn't think a serious story would sell newspapers. He concentrated on Mary Thomas who told Whearley that earth was populated with all the undesirables of other planets. The ones in the saucers were 5,000 years ahead of us in culture and they were here to show us the way. Others at the meeting tried to point out to Whearley that not all members of the group were as avid believers as Mary. Most were open minded, ready to rationally consider all possibilities.

The speaker for the evening was Air Force Major Robert C. Gardner. Gardner, who held two college degrees and a California teacher's credential, said he based his knowledge of UFOs from those "who knew the score." He cited retired Air Force General Benjamin Chidlaw who told Gardner he had lost many officers and planes trying to contact UFOs. Gardner said the government had captured flying saucers but powerful interests had kept a lid on the news. Reporter Whearley refused to take Gardner seriously, despite Gardner's credentials. It wouldn't be until 1978 when nuclear physicist Stanton T. Friedman took it upon himself to release what was known about the captured flying saucer which allegedly crashed at Roswell in 1947 that reporters became less dismissive.

The Long Beach UFO Research Society, of which Reverend Carl Anderson was president, also hosted a number of "interesting" speakers including Kelvin Rowe, author of *A Call at Dawn: A message from our brothers of the planets Pluto and Jupiter* (1958) which described face-to-face meetings with inhabitants of other planets. His contacts began with voices...voices he heard while driving near Mt. Palomar from a construction job...but there was no one there. He mentioned this to a friend George Adamski who told him not to worry; Adamski's contact with aliens had started the same way (Adamski wrote about his encounters in a 1953 book *Flying Saucers Have Landed*). The voices spoke in English, just like they had to Reverend Anderson, but Rowe couldn't understand what they were talking about. His first physical encounter was while he was working in the desert. Others also observed the crafts which numbered around five.

In August 1958, the UFO Research Society (which had taken on a new name – the Cosmic Research Society) hosted Trevor James Constable, author of *They Live in the Sky*. Constable (who wrote under the pseudonym Trevor James) believed that UFOs came from a parallel universe known as Etheria and that there were two categories of UFO, some were machines and others living creatures. These invisible creatures he called "Sky Critters" and they lived in the atmosphere, but were invisible to normal sight. When these sky creatures, which Constable said were biological organisms native to our atmosphere, entered the spectrum of visible light, they appeared as rapidly moving, pulsating light sources which were often confused with the interdimensional machines known as flying saucers.

In the summer of 1957, Constable used infrared-sensitive black and white film to record these creatures. He enticed them by using a meditation practice he labeled the Star Exercise. With this exercise he aligned his body with the earth's magnetic field, while setting himself up to become a "bioenergetics beacon" to attract the inquisitive creatures into the recordable ranges of his infrared camera. It evidently worked. By mid-1958 Constable had captured over 100 anomalous images on film which he published in his 1976 book *The Cosmic Pulse of Life*. (You can see some examples on the Internet at tarrdaniel.com/documents/Ufology/skycritters.html). Some showed dark objects, others showed ellipses that looked like living cells, while still others resembled more classic UFOs.

The Long Beach press loved to poke fun at Long Beach's UFO groups, especially their more "offbeat" speakers. One such speaker was Clint Cary who addressed the Long Beach Interplanetary Research Group in January 1960. Cary's claim to fame was painting pictures "telepathized" from the planet Rillispore which revolved around the star-sun Rigel in the constellation of Orion. He also told the audience he had made two trips to Rillispore in a flying saucer which was a mile in diameter and 800 feet thick and capable of carrying 500 Rillisporians. The Rillisporians were six to seven feet tall, Cary said, and were hermaphroditic, each person being a perfect blend of masculine and feminine.

Cary told those attending the lecture at Morgan Hall that he first met the aliens at a deserted ranch in the high desert. This was some time after they had sent him a "telepathogram" in Mexico

City, telling him to stop his career as a trombone player and become an artist. Why was he chosen above all humans? Cary said it was because he had a perfect balance between positive and negative elements, and the Rillisporians knew he wouldn't come back and set up a church to worship alien doctrines. He said the trips to Rillispore only took three days because the planet was in the fifth dimension; he also learned that Einstein was wrong. Light was round, it didn't really travel at all – it was the only fixed thing in the universe.

The finale of Cary's lecture was the unveiling of the paintings he said he had painted telepathically. The hall lights were dimmed and the paintings of alien cities and alien life were illuminated by ultraviolet light. In actuality he had pioneered what became known as "Black Light Art," using fluorescent paint on fiberglass. At his Long Beach lecture, Cary went on to add that when he showed the paintings in Nashville, Tennessee, a little old lady was levitated three feet off the floor. No such thing happened in Long Beach.

Interestingly none of these paintings remain. In 2009 Chris Holly writing for *UFO and Paranormal News from Around the World* tried to locate Cary's "telepathized" paintings. She interviewed a woman who had seen the paintings and described them as "extremely beautiful and without question one of a kind pieces of art." Though Holly found later pieces of Cary's work, she could not find one sample or copy of any of Cary's extensive alien pieces. Chris Holly wrote: "I found it odd that I was not able to find one of these paintings anywhere or in any article written about this man. It seems all his incredible paintings of alien life and cities are lost. I tried, but found them impossible to find."

Long Beach reporters weren't as dismissive as they were with the UFO Research Society and Interplanetary Research Group when telling of three Lakewood Plaza housewives and a dozen neighborhood kids who saw strange objects dancing beneath the clouds in December 1957.

Evelyn Dilley had just gotten off a bus around 4 p.m. when she happened to glance upward and spotted some mysterious objects; she kept looking skyward to see if they were still there as she walked to her home. Along the way she called to neighbor Edna Anderson who also saw the objects. Another neighbor, Anne Palmer, looked out her window and saw Edna and Evelyn staring at the sky. She went outside, looked up, and saw the objects. Kids in the area also joined in watching.

Evelyn Dilley had been a skeptic about flying saucers but couldn't explain what she saw. She observed five objects and she was positive they weren't planes, weather balloons, kites or birds. They had a glow to them, like a light bulb. She described them as moving in tight formation, flying tight circles beneath the clouds as if they were being whirled around on the end of a yoyo string. Suddenly they would shoot straight up into the clouds, out of sight. They kept doing this for about 10 minutes until they disappeared into a cloud and did not reappear. They looked like pie plates, and no sound accompanied their rapid movement. Evelyn Dilley wasn't sure what they were, but was hoping for a logical explanation. None came.

Long Beach finally hired a reporter who didn't scoff at UFOs. George Robeson, an Air Force veteran, had talked to many jet pilots who saw and chased objects they were unable to apprehend. After one Air Force interrogation, many of the pilots vowed they would never report another UFO even if it landed on the wing of their aircraft! They had been made to feel like fools by those in command. George Robeson also found librarians were a pretty reliable source of information.

Long Beach librarian Ruth Austin was sitting in her back yard at 21st and Locust on September 21, 1965, Robeson told readers. It was around 8 or 8:30 p.m. when Ruth saw what appeared to be a flight of birds because of the wavering pattern of their flight. But it didn't behave like a flock of birds because it moved so fast it remained in her field of vision only three or four seconds. Also, each object in the flight glowed with a soft light, as if illuminated from within. Her fellow librarian, Dorothy Piper, saw the flight return a few moments later. The return flight was in a loose V-formation. The first formation was compact, according to Ruth Austin. About a half minute later, both women saw a single illuminated flying object, apparently a straggler tailing the rest of the gang. It too zipped out of sight in a matter of seconds.

Being librarians, they sought out every plausible explanation. At first they thought a spotlight had been focused on a flock of birds, but they abandoned that idea because there had been no visible beam. They consider the possibility that a number of birds had eaten some phosphorescent material in the sea. They weren't too sure about that explanation. Ruth Austin confessed to Robeson (perhaps because he took her seriously) that she had seen a similar phenomenon two years earlier, about the same time of year – a single object this time, maybe a bird, and it glowed. She hadn't reported it because she didn't want the public to think that librarians were "kooks."

Reporter Robeson, however, did not think Austin was a "kook." He reported Austin's sighting to the Air Force. On August 3, 1966 he wrote:

I suppose I did my old outfit dirt when I reported UFO sightings off the Long Beach coastline last year by two of our most stable and scholarly librarians, who are not, as far as I know, given to hallucinations. The Air Force invariably shrugs the whole thing off with comments such as 'a little swamp-gas.' If there are no swamps in the vicinity of the sighting, USAF can call it 'stomach gas' and who is to say it isn't.

On May 5, 1961, the Cold War became a little more balanced when the United States put its first man, Alan Shepard, into space. Fearful of Russian superiority in space exploration, the United States was catching up. But how far ahead were the Russians? Could those UFOs seen by many actually be Soviet craft?

In January 1961, *Press-Telegram* reporter Bob Beckman decided to do a survey of all 55 known UFO sighters in the area to see if they still believed what they observed were really unidentified objects.

Forty responded to the questionnaire. The only unanimous answer given by those questioned was that once a person saw an unidentified flying object it remained vividly in one's memory forever. Eighty-three per cent of the sighters said they wouldn't report a sighting if they saw another disc because they were met with disbelief and scorn. Seventy-five percent of those answering were as sure today, or more so, that what they saw could not be explained away as natural phenomena.

Two sighters responding to the survey claimed they were not sure about what they saw, stating that their sighting could perhaps have been explained logically. Six others, although not specifying why, simply stated what they saw probably wasn't a flying saucer.

What did they see? Descriptions ranged from cigar-like objects to lights of changing color. Seventeen sighters believed their UFOs were oval. Eleven said the object they saw was more like a cigar. Nine witnessed strange lights hovering or moving swiftly through the sky. Three saw "oversized" stars move erratically. Twelve observed red objects and seven saw white ones. One woman said the object she viewed was a deep blue. Twenty responded that the color of the object they saw changed at regular intervals.

Only one sighting was made in the morning and two in the afternoon. Fourteen sightings in the Long Beach area were between midnight and dawn. Twelve were seen between nightfall and midnight and eleven at dusk.

The survey also revealed eighteen of the forty UFOs were headed eastward over Long Beach. Eight were speeding southeastward, seven northeastward, five northwest and two southward. Seventeen of those responding believed the saucers were intelligently controlled. Seven of the seventeen were convinced Venus was their point of origin. Twenty-three either left the questionnaire space blank or admitted they didn't know where the UFO came from. None of those queried believed the UFOs were from Russia.

Eleven of the forty Long Beach area residents were repeat sighters. Ten saw their second mysterious object either hovering over the area or racing from horizon to horizon. One person claimed he had seen two additional UFOs since making his first report twelve years earlier. Only one of the repeat sighters reported their second sighting.

Bob Beckman also recounted what Lt. Col. Lawrence J. Tacker said in his publication *Flying Saucers and the U.S. Air Force*. Besides being weather balloons, birds or aircraft, Tacker offered another explanation: "Occasionally, objects that exist on the surface of the eye may be mistaken for distant objects. Many reported unidentified objects are nothing more than minute blood capillaries on the surface of the retina of the eye." Tucker believed that the flying saucer era was coming to an end. Air Force statistics showed only 364 UFOs reported in 1959, compared to 1,501 in 1952 and 1,178 in 1947.

Sightings did appear to decrease after 1960. There was the librarians' sighting in 1965, discussed earlier, and a brief mention in June 1966 of a dozen witnesses claiming to have seen flying saucers over Lakewood and Bellflower. Was it because people were too embarrassed to report what they saw? Such was not the case with Wilmington security guard Jack Hill.

Hill said he didn't believe in UFOs but he knew he saw something strange in the early morning hours of July 18, 1967. At 3:50 a.m., bicycling around the Consolidated Lumber Yard, making his rounds, he spotted an elongated object 80 to 100 feet long and 20 or 30 feet deep that seemed to emit a soft bluish-green light. The windowless object hovered 50 feet in the air and Hill wasn't about to let it "park" at the lumberyard without permission so he fired six rounds into the object, putting its lights out. Even without the lights he could see the object was still there, then it started going straight up as Hill continued to fire, speeding out of sight in a westerly direction toward San Pedro. He was sure it wasn't an airplane or helicopter – it had no propellers or rotors, and was soundless when it hovered. When it sped away it made no more noise than a car motor idling.

When Hill reported the shooting to the police, since it was against the law to fire weapons in Wilmington, they asked him why he opened fire. He told them he was a guard and he took his job seriously. When he was at work no one came into the yard without permission. He also thought if he immobilized the object by shooting out its engine, there would be no question about UFOs. Police agreed the isolated location would make an ideal landing spot for a UFO - there was a large open yard with an asphalt area and no overhead wires to hamper a landing.

Following Hill's story in the newspaper, the harbor division police station was overwhelmed with panicky people. Calls ran a gamut from simple requests for more information to ideas for staking out the lumber yard in case the UFO returned. Hill, too, was overwhelmed with callers. Later, after much thought and some sleep, Hill admitted the saucer could have been a weather balloon. He also admitted the four bullets he showed the media were only slugs from target practice on a hunting trip, he had produced them to embellish his story about firing at the object.

By 1969 Air Force rocket tests were given as an explanation for UFOs. In June 1984 the first U.S. satellite was launched into orbit around the earth with many more to follow. Several "strange" sightings were later dismissed as simple satellites spotted from earth. But UFOs are still being sighted, as a search through the Internet will show.

Many present day UFO believers present interesting evidence that there is a UFO base located underwater in the Catalina channel off the Southern California coast. Reporters for the *Press-Telegram* in 1954 seemed to have missed this intriguing possibility. It wouldn't be until fifty-two years later that another *Press-Telegram* columnist, Kristopher Hanson, would uncover the story of the Japanese ship *Aliki*.

In January 2007, Hanson contacted UFO researcher Preston Dennett who had written about the *Aliki* which, while off the coast of Long Beach on August 8, 1954, encountered an underwater UFO. The intercepted radio message from the ship read: "Saw fireball move in and out of sea without being doused. Left wake of white smoke; course erratic; vanished from sight."

Hanson also reached out to Lt. Chuck Engbring of the U.S. Coast Guard. Engbring remembered an instance where several passengers on a flight out of LAX reported seeing a UFO ascend from the sea to the sky off Point Vicente in Rancho Palos Verdes. Hanson next contacted

Sharon Diggs-Jackson, the Long Beach Airport spokesperson, to see if she had received any reports of mysterious UFOs. She had. In December 2006, a resident reported seeing erratic lights moving through the sky which airport officials could not explain.

Perhaps the most well-known recent sighting came from the Long Beach Police Department. It was around 11:30 p.m. on December 25, 2004, when the police helicopter's video camera recorded a glowing object floating through the Long Beach sky. Unable to identify it, they sent the tape to local military officials. One theory was that it was a prank candle balloon, especially common in the 1960s after how to build one was described in a science magazine. The pilot's best guess was that it was a bag or balloon with a flare attached to it, which would explain the trailing sulfur-like light. In the video the brilliantly lit object looked as though it was traveling fast, but it could just have been the effect of the helicopter orbiting the item at a high rate of speed with the background flashing by. The military could not say definitively what the object was. A copy of the tape was given to a local television station and broadcast around the world, the earlier theories were dismissed. Nobody could figure out what it was.

So are UFOs real? In 1994, several government intelligence memos were declassified. The most alarming fact kept secret about Roswell was revealed – inside the flying saucer Russian writing in block letters from the Cyrillic alphabet had been stamped in a ring running around the inside of the craft. It appeared the Russians had gotten hold of German technology involving a fast flying aircraft shaped like a saucer. Two aerospace engineers, brothers Walter and Reimar Horten, had invented several of Hitler's flying-wing aircraft, including one called the Horten 229 or Horten IX, a wing-shaped, tailless airplane that had been developed at a secret facility in Baden-Baden during World War II. It appeared Stalin had gotten control of the Horten's blueprints and plans. One memo revealed the flying disc that crashed at Roswell was more advanced than anything American scientists had ever seen; most importantly it had appeared on Army radar screens briefly then suddenly disappeared.

What about the child-size pilots inside the flying disc? According to a former engineer who worked for defense contractor Edgerton, Germeshausen, and Grier (EG&G), the aviators were not aliens. The engineer was told they were created to look like them by Josef Mengele, the Nazi officer who experimented on humans during World War II, shortly before or immediately after the war. The craft was piloted remotely, and the child-sized creatures simply props to scare Americans.

EG&G engineers were told that part of Joseph Stalin's offer to Mengele after the war stated that if he could create a crew of grotesque, child-size aviators for Stalin, Mengele would be given a laboratory in which to continue his work. According to information revealed to the engineers, Mengele held up his side of the bargain and provided Stalin with the child-size crew. Stalin did not honor his commitment. Mengele never moved to the Soviet Union. Instead, he lived for four years in Germany under an assumed name and then escaped to South America, where he lived first in Argentina and then in Paraguay, until his death in 1979. When Stalin sent the reengineered children in the craft over New Mexico, hoping it would land there, the engineers were told Stalin's plan was for the children to climb out and be mistaken for visitors from Mars. Panic would ensue, just like it did after the radio broadcast of *The War of the Worlds*. From this President Truman would see how easily the totalitarian dictator could control the masses using propaganda.

Annie Jacobsen in her book *Area 51* asked the sole surviving engineer from EG&G why Truman didn't reveal the truth in 1947. Jacobsen was told the United States was doing the same thing - experimenting on humans – and didn't want the fact to come out. Was it true?

Reporter Eileen Welsome uncovered information that the Atomic Energy Commission (AEC) began experiments on humans in 1951 and continued through the 1980s. In 1993, Welsome wrote a newspaper story stating the AEC had conducted plutonium experiments on human beings, most notably retarded children and orphan boys from the Fernald State School, outside Boston, without the children's or their guardians' knowledge or consent.

In the spring of 1994, *60 Minutes* aired a program about a young boy, Dwayne Sexton, with leukemia. In 1968, Dwayne was taken to a specially designed radiation therapy chamber at a clinic run by the Atomic Energy Commission. What the boy's parents didn't know at the time, and what was later uncovered by reporter Howard Rosenberg was that Dwayne was being steered away from conventional chemotherapy, which was not nearly as effective for childhood leukemia then as it is today, so that he could be used as part of a human experiment being conducted on behalf of NASA and the Pentagon to determine how much radiation an astronaut or soldier could withstand and still function. Young Dwayne Sexton died, as did all the children who were treated at the AEC clinic with total body irradiation.

Upon hearing of these horrible revelations, President Clinton opened an investigation to look into what the AEC had done and the secrets it had kept, but according to Annie Jacobsen's source, the AEC kept most of the information from the president.

What of the flying saucer remains? Unclassified documents revealed they would stay at Wright-Patterson Air Force Base until 1955, when the secret military installation, Area 51, came into being. The base had many purposes besides housing the Roswell remains. It appeared the CIA wanted to establish a secret CIA test facility to build a new spy plane which would keep watch over the Soviet Union's burgeoning nuclear weapons program. It was here the U-2, and later the A-12 Oxcart and the D-21 drone was developed.

As soon as the U-2s started flying out of Area 51, reports of UFO sightings by airline pilots and air traffic controllers skyrocketed. Later painted black to blend in with the sky, the U-2s at that time were silver, which meant their long, shiny wings reflected light down from the upper atmosphere in a way that led citizens all over California, Nevada, and Utah to think the planes were UFOs. By 1957, according to the CIA monograph *CIA's Role in the Study of UFOs*, the U-2s accounted for more than half of all UFO sightings reported in the continental United States. What else went on at Area 51? It may be many more years before we know – everything that has happened at Area 51 since 1968 remains classified.

Could other UFO sightings be attributed to the testing of new types of airplanes, such as the strange looking Horton Wingless Airplane once housed at the Long Beach airport? Designed by William Horton in 1954, the strange looking craft was called a flying what-is-it. It had a big, squat body like a manta ray, no fuselage, a needle nose and no wings, except for a couple of dinky little stubs that looked as if they couldn't even support a bird. Horton made amazing claims for his unconventional plane, convincing many it carried double the payload of a regular plane and took off in much less space. He also said it cost about half as much to build, but he didn't have the money to develop it. Howard Hughes was interested in Horton's craft, but the venture failed not because the airplane didn't fly, but because Hughes wanted to take full credit for the patents and production rights, which Horton refused to do. A vindictive Hughes slapped a law suit on Horton that stopped production. However the craft did fly as several YouTube videos show.

Many questioned what was going on with the military at the Long Beach Municipal Airport. The military had had a presence in town since April 1928 when the U.S. Naval Air Reserves moved to the air field; the Army Air Corps Reserves joined them in 1929 and in 1931 the regular U.S. Army and Navy Air Forces chose Long Beach as their home base. The navy moved to Los Alamitos in May 1942, but the army would remain at the Long Beach air field until October 1960. The airport was also home to a weather station, validating the weather balloon explanation, the most frequent explanation given by authorities. However, many wondered, with Douglas Aircraft next to the airport, if Douglas was being used to build and test secret military aircraft.

It seems certain that some UFO sightings could be attributed to secretive testing of aircraft. Were the Russians really behind the 1947 Roswell crash as revealed in declassified 1994 intelligence memos? Could the alleged Roswell aliens really have been genetically altered humans? Was more going on at the Army Air Force base at the Long Beach Airport than the military wanted the public to know?

One United States Senator, Harry Reid of Nevada, also had unanswered questions about UFOs. On December 16, 2017, the *New York Times* reported on the once classified project that Reid and his friend, Robert Bigelow, the billionaire founder of an aerospace company, set up.

Reid, the *Times* said, was also supported in his efforts to fund the program by the late Senators Ted Stevens of Alaska, Daniel Inouye of Hawaii, and John Glenn of Ohio, the first American to orbit the Earth, who told Reid the federal government should take a serious look at UFOs. The four senators were aware that many sightings were not reported up the military's chain of command because service members were afraid they would be laughed at or stigmatized. Ted Stevens, who had been a pilot in the Army's air force, flying transport missions over China during World War II, told Reid he had once been tailed by a strange aircraft with no known origin, which he said had followed his plane for miles.

Working to keep a program that he was sure would draw scrutiny from others, Reid said he, Stevens and Inouye (Glenn had left the Senate in 1999) made sure there was never any public debate about the program on the Senate floor during budget debates. "This was so-called black money," Reid told the *Times* regarding the Defense Department budget for classified programs. In the $600 billion annual Defense Department budget, the $22 million spent on the Advanced Aerospace Threat Identification Program was almost impossible to find – which was how the Pentagon wanted it.

For years the program, run by military intelligence official Luis Elizondo, investigated reports of unidentified flying objects. Among the anomalies the program studied were video and audio recordings of aerial encounters by military pilots and unknown objects. In one instance, the program looked at 2004 video footage of a Navy F/A-18 Super Hornet surrounded by a glowing object of unknown origin traveling at a high rate of speed in a location that officials declined to identify.

Until the *New York Times* article, the Defense Department never acknowledged the existence of the program, which intelligence sources said began in 2007 and shut down in 2012. Most of the money went to an aerospace research company run by Robert Bigelow. Bigelow Aerospace, which is working with NASA to produce expandable craft for humans to use in space, hired subcontractors and solicited research for the program.

Under Bigelow's direction, the company modified buildings in Las Vegas for the storage of metal alloys and other materials that Luis Elizondo and program contractors said had been recovered from unidentified aerial phenomena. "We're sort of in the position of what would happen if you gave Leonardo da Vinci a garage-door opener," said Harold E. Puthoff, an engineer who worked as a contractor for the program. "First of all, he'd try to figure out what is this plastic stuff. He wouldn't know anything about the electromagnetic signals involved or its function."

Researchers also studied people who said they had experienced physical effects from encounters with the objects and examined them for any physiological changes. In addition, investigators spoke to military service members who had reported sightings of strange aircraft. Bigelow's Las Vegas-based company also examined documents that described sightings of aircraft that seemed to move at very high velocities with no visible signs of propulsion, or that hovered with no apparent means of lift.

In an interview reported by the *Times*, Bigelow stated that the United States was the most backward country in the world on the issue of UFOs. The nation's scientists were scared of being ostracized, and our media afraid of the stigma. China and Russia, Bigelow went on, were much more open and had established huge organizations within their countries to study the issue. Even smaller countries like Belgium, France, England and South American countries like Chile were more open, than the United States.

The Advanced Aviation Threat Identification Program ended in 2012 because the Department of Defense determined there were other, higher priority issues that merited funding. But its backers claim that the program remains in existence despite lack of money. For the past five years, they say, officials with the program have continued to investigate episodes brought to them by service members, while also carrying out their other Defense Department duties.

In an interview with the *Times*, Luis Elizondo, who resigned as project director in October 2017 because of his frustration with the limitations placed on the program, said he and his government colleagues had determined that the phenomena they had studied did not seem to originate from any country. "That fact is not something any government or institution should classify in order to keep secret from the people," he said.

For his part, Harry Reid said he did not know where the objects had come from. "If anyone says they have the answers now, they're fooling themselves," he said. "We do not know." But, he said, "We have to start someplace."

As they say in the X-files "The Truth is Out There." But where to find it and who to believe, remains unanswered.

Spys?

Things hadn't been easy for Ruby Smith since her aviator husband Bill was reported missing over China in 1948. Unable to find a decent place to rent because of the Southern California housing crisis, she tried to purchase a two-bedroom pink stucco house at 141 W. 51st Street in North Long Beach in October 1948 for $9200. Though she put up $1600, the sale couldn't go through because she didn't have the power of attorney for her husband or his signature on certain documents. But how could she? He was missing. She didn't know if he was dead or alive.

Ruby, however, never gave up hope that her husband was still alive. The government and her friends tried to warn her as gently as possible that Bill might have been killed or died in prison, but she refused to believe he was dead. The reason? He had promised that if he died he would come back to her. He never came, so she knew he hadn't died.

For over a year Ruby Smith anxiously awaited news of her husband. Finally, just after Christmas 1949, Mrs. Smith received word that Bill Smith had been a prisoner of the Chinese for thirteen months. He and fellow pilot Elmer Bender would be released if two conditions were met: Smith and Bender had to admit they had been spying for the United States and the United States had to officially recognize the Red Chinese government as the legitimate ruling body of China.

Senator Eugene McCarthy accused the Truman administration of "deceit and dishonesty" in dealing with the release of the prisoners.

McCarthy, a former Marine, favored "doing anything, including forceful means, to go in and get" the two captives. Would the United States go to war to free Smith and Bender? It wouldn't have to, thanks to a "fake" confession and the help of the British who agreed, as one of the Chinese concessions, to recognize the Red government if the Chinese released the U.S. aviators.

On May 19, 1950, all of American shouted with joy as a Douglas Skymaster roared in from Hawaii bringing home to Long Beach William Smith and Elmer Bender who had been held captive by Chinese Communists for nearly 19 months. The pair's airplane had been forced down in Communist China on October 19, 1948, and the men charged with spying. Bender and Smith, however, had a different story to tell.

The pair said they had merely been on a routine flight, so Bender could get in required flying time, when they managed to get over Chinese territory by mistake. As fate would have it, their engine failed and they were forced to land in China, thus beginning their long captivity. The two emphasized their flight was definitely an innocent affair, with no cameras or special equipment on board; they swore they had not even realized they had crossed over into Communist China.

Upon their return to Long Beach, Navy Chief William C. Smith and Master Sergeant Elmer C. Bender admitted they won their liberty only when they signed a "fabricated statement" hinting at espionage. They signed it only after becoming convinced that no effort was being made to free them by United States officials. They considered it a statement, rather than a confession. It was the only way they could think of to see their families again.

Ten years later, in October 1959, August and Ida Langelle were alarmed when their son Russell was accused by the Russians of being an American spy. Would he be held prisoner or even executed? The North Long Beach couple (266 E. 65th Way) prayed the United States government could negotiate his release.

Russell A. Langelle was chief security officer of the U.S. Embassy in Moscow when he was targeted by the Soviets and charged with espionage. On October 16, 1959, both he and a U.S. mole Colonel Pyotr Popov were arrested by the KGB.

The U.S. refuted all charges against Langelle and accused Russia of seizing the security officer and trying to force him by threats and bribery into becoming a spy for the Soviets. The State Department charged that Soviet police kidnapped the 37-year-old American embassy official, threatening him and his family with physical violence and tried to bribe him to spy for the Russians. The Russians strongly disagreed. They claimed Langelle had been involved in receiving information from Russian Colonel Pyotr Popov who had been recruited by the U.S. to spy on the Reds.

Years later the true story was revealed. It appeared that Langelle was indeed in contact with Soviet agent Pyotr Popov. Popov had volunteered to spy for the United States in 1953. He was angry at what he felt was Soviet exploitation of Russian peasants, including his own family. For six years he provided the CIA with valuable information, but was arrested in 1959 after receiving a letter from U.S. authorities the Soviets were able to decipher. Put in prison, the Soviets used every means at their disposal to convince Popov to become a double agent. Popov seemingly agreed, but he was able to pass one last message to the Americans.

The KGB had sent him to a meeting with Russell Langelle in Moscow. The pair met on a bus, and in full view of KGB surveillance, Popov shook Langelle's hand and managed to slip him a note, rolled in a cylinder the size of a cigarette, revealing that the Soviets knew of Popov's defection. The cylinder message provided a detailed account of the KGB's knowledge of Popov's cooperation with the Americans and their plans to exploit him in the future. He had painstakingly written the message while in prison, over a number of months, concealing it under a bandage he had obtained by purposely cutting his finger. Later, the KGB realized they had been duped. Langelle was expelled from Russia and Popov sent to a Soviet firing squad.

Langelle and his family were sent home for their safety and to keep U.S.-Soviet relations on a somewhat even keel. Langelle's mother Ida, and sister Marie Sellman, were happy to have him home.

His mother told the *Press-Telegram* she hadn't wanted her son to go to Russia in the first place, but was happy Russell had been able to travel to Long Beach earlier that year (1960) and see his father, August, shortly before his father died.

At a news conference Langelle expressed the belief that the Russians expelled him because of his zeal in protecting the American Embassy against Soviet penetration efforts. The fact that American authorities absolved top Kremlin officials of blame in the case indicated that the United States did not want the episode to interfere with Cold War peace talks.

What Langelle did after returning to the United States is somewhat sketchy, however the April 10, 1960 *Press-Telegram* mentioned Langelle had a new State Department security job, acting as chief bodyguard and companion for visiting heads of state. In *The Man Who Kew Too Much* author Dick Russell writes that this State Department job was actually a CIA cover assignment. In 1963, Russell asserts, Langelle was assigned to the Western Hemisphere Section of the Operations Branch of the Soviet Russia Division, and involved in keeping track of Lee Harvey Oswald. Did Langelle know about Oswald's plans to assassinate President John F. Kennedy? Many believe he did. The debate still lingers.

It wasn't until 1964, when KGB agent Major Yuri Nosenko defected, that the CIA learned how the KGB had allegedly monitored Popov's movement. Nosenko had defected to the United States just after the assassination of President Kennedy, bearing details of Lee Oswald's time in the U.S.S.R. Many had thought Popov had been betrayed by other agents. That was not the case...according to Nosenko it was through the use of a chemical. Nosenko reported that Langelle's Russian maid had dusted the diplomat's shoes with a traceable substance. The KGB using a sniffer dog, tracked Langelle to a mailbox where the police found a note he had mailed to Popov. Others do not believe Nosenko's story.

The Korean War

While the Navy was gearing down after the end of World War II, closing the local Navy hospital and shipyard, and chasing UFOs, world events were triggering another war. Many thought it would be with China, but diplomacy solved that crisis; this was not to be the case in Korea. The world was much different than it had been at the start of the last war. In August 1945 nuclear bombs, very small by the standard of what would come, killed more than 100,000 and injured and sickened countless more, and left Hiroshima and Nagasaki, Japan, in ruins. The world had entered the Atomic Age. Many wondered if these devices would again be used in this war.

On June 25, 1950, North Korean Communist troops invaded South Korea. On June 27th President Truman, responding to the U.N. plea for member nations to aid their invaded ally, ordered U.S. air and naval forces to help defend South Korea. By the 30th Truman had ordered U.S. ground troops to the scene. The president had avoided war with China over the Bender and Smith episode, but now the Korean War had started and the United States drawn into it because of its ties with the United Nations.

On June 28, 1950, the commander of the Long Beach Naval Station issued orders to tighten security and take precautions against sabotage. This was hard to do because many of the workers from the Navy shipyard, which was closing July 1, 1950, had already transferred to the Navy station and there hadn't been enough time to issue them proper passes. But plans for war moved quickly. All leaves were cancelled and by July 1st naval vessels were already on their way to Korea.

On July 11th, Douglas Aircraft was awarded an $8 million Air Force contract to recondition a fleet of mothballed B-26 attack bombers. This was great news for the company which would add 1500 workers to its current crew of 7000. The 2500 B-26s built in Long Beach by Douglas during World War II were originally known as A-26 Invaders. The plane was recognized for its long range, high speed and heavy firepower and was designed especially for offensive action against ground installations. It was the fastest U.S. bomber of the last war and it was hoped it would live up to its past performance record in this one.

Selective Service boards also swung into action calling in the first group of draftees. On September 28, 1950, one hundred seven Long Beach men left for basic training at Fort Ord. Volunteer plane spotters, needed to supplement radar warning systems which couldn't pick up low-flying aircraft, were recruited for service and assigned to the reactivated aircraft observation post in the tower of the Villa Riviera.

The war ended quickly for some men. On August 7, 1950, Jordan High School graduate John LaVern Johnson of 665 Silva became the first Long Beach man killed in Korea. Another Long Beach Marine, 20-year-old Long Beach Marine Corporal Ronald Lee Keller, of 22 39th Place, was killed the following day. For some, such as Sergeant Johnny J. Martin, the war only lasted 45 minutes. Martin, a Marine who earned a Purple Heart, lost his right arm minutes after hitting the Korean beach at Inchon. The 24-year-old had also won a Bronze Star on Saipan during World War II. Wounded in September, he made it home to Long Beach in time for the birth of daughter Christy Lynn born on December 30, 1950.

Long Beach Fire Captain Robert N. Maddux, in charge of crash crews at Long Beach Municipal Airport, lost part of his ear and found out the hard way that Marine sentries took their job seriously. On December 18, 1950, Maddux was out fishing with his nephew.

Heading back to their boat landing near Sam's Sea Food Restaurant in Sunset Beach they passed under the bridge over Pacific Coast Highway where a sentry at the Naval Ammunition and Net Depot in Seal Beach was posted. When the sentry yelled at them they shut off the motor and drifted back toward him to hear what he was saying. The 17-year-old guard fired, striking Maddux. Maddux fell over into the boat but managed to stand up with the help of his nephew, Robert Simmons. The two threw up their hands but the sentry fired at them twice more, missing both times.

The Navy offered no apologies. The sentry had just been doing his job. Maddux and Simmons were in a restricted area and boats using the inlet had to have a permit from the ammunition depot for each trip. The two didn't have a permit and had failed to stop when guards hailed them on their way out of Anaheim Bay. With thousands of tons of explosives in all shapes and sizes the Navy couldn't afford to relax its vigil against possible sabotage.

On June 9, 1950, Brigadier General Luther W. Sweetser Jr., commanding general of the 452nd Air Force Bomb Wing at the Long Beach Municipal Airport, received his orders. The 452nd was being reactivated. There had been a contest of sorts going on with the 448th, also at the Long Beach airport, to see which would be the first called up to full strength (the training centers at Long Beach and Chicago were the only two reserve centers in the U.S. which had two bomb wings). But the 452nd had a higher honor – it was the first Air Force Reserve unit in the United States to obtain 100 percent status. Little did they realize this also meant they would be the first to go to Korea. On July 29, 1950, they received orders calling them up for active duty. All were reservists, coming from communities throughout the area. They were used to training one week each month at the Long Beach Air Force base at the airport, now they had twelve days to get their personal lives straightened out before being sent to battle.

Three months to the day after they were called to active duty, Long Beach's own 452nd Bomb Wing roared into action over Korea. Their training had been limited to only four hours a month to maintain their proficiency in all types of flying, instrument formation, bomb runs and plain straight flying. Supplies were scarce and some of their B-26 bombers had been cannibalized to keep others in the air. They also had to buy their own parachutes from surplus stores. Similarly they purchased heated flying suits for the cold Korean winters. Then, with hastily improvised canvas gas tanks shoved into the bomb bays of the B26s, they flew out over the Pacific and into combat.

It was a frustrating fight – they flew up the Yalu River and were allowed to bomb one side of the river and not the other. Russian MIG fighters came out of the sanctuary of the north side of the river and did considerable damage to the B26s. But some American planes always managed to smash through despite the odds. It was Sergeant Clifford Hubbard of 3556 Wise Avenue who was credited with shooting down the first enemy plane on November 5th. The first casualty was Corporal Billie L. King, a gunner with the 452nd killed on December 17 by Korean fire. During their first two months of combat, the 452nd flew 300 missions and 1,150 sorties, destroying 1,183 enemy buildings, 59 railroad cars, 25 trucks, 8 warehouses, 3 tanks, one gasoline dump and one oil-storage dump. About 859 enemy troops were killed.

With two air wings, the Long Beach Air Force base at the Municipal Airport was one of the largest in the nation. In March 1951 members of the 448th strode through the gates of the Long Beach Air base to report for active duty. Among the nearly 1000 members of the Wing were 30 in the Women's Air Force. As they gathered together they heard some disarming news: the 448th was being disbanded. They had all been assigned to other units at seven other stations throughout the country. Many would join the 22nd and 44th Bomb Wings flying B-29s at March Field in Riverside.

In May 1951, wives and mothers of men in the 452nd Bomb Wing began their own campaign, "bombing" Washington with letters and telegrams protesting what they described as "inequitable treatment" of the 452nd. The women were angry the Air Force refused the men permission to return home, although many had completed 60 or more missions and no replacement forces were in place. During World War II 50 missions was the norm for rotation, but now no one seemed to know what the rules were. The women complained that the men's morale had hit bottom. All had fought in the last war, were married, and missed their wives and children. None knew when they would be returning home. The women's campaign paid off. In June 1951, a rotation program for 452nd Bomb Wing air crew members began. However, many wives and relatives were indignant over the fact that it did not apply to ground crews and continued to press for action.

On May 9, 1952, the wing was officially out of the war and reverted to reserve status at the Long Beach Airport. The men had served on active duty for 21 months, first in Japan and later in Pusan, Korea. Their efforts were appreciated. In February 1952, the Republic of Korea issued the unit a citation for "exceptional meritorious service" in combating the Communist aggression. They were also honored with a U.S. Presidential Unit Citation. Korea again paid them homage in August 1953 awarding the unit the Korean Presidential Award. Long Beach's old 452nd Bomb Wing (L) was deactivated in Korea. In its place, the 452nd Tactical Reconnaissance Wing was activated in Long Beach with mostly new personnel. The purpose of the newly named unit was to photograph enemy installations on which tactical units could plan day-to-day operations. Later it became the 452nd Troop Carrier Wing which ultimately moved to March Air Force Base.

The Korean War had a profound effect on Long Beach. Many businesses and city departments lost men called up for service. The good news was that the military cut-backs which the city experienced in 1950 were rescinded; perhaps the greatest economic boom was the reopening of the Navy shipyard.

The Korean War caught the military off guard. They had to quickly reactivate many of the support services they had done away with after World War II. One of the casualties had been the Long Beach Navy Shipyard. Since the yard had been closed such a short time, none of the equipment had been salvaged or the buildings dismantled. The major obstacle, however, was that it was sinking because of all the oil taken out of the ground around Terminal Island.

Congress soon remedied this by appropriating $1.5 million in federal funds for help with subsidence.

There was much to celebrate on Navy Day, February 1, 1951, in Long Beach and the rest of Southern California. The first important event was the opening of the Naval Supply Depot in San Pedro, which had been moved to San Pedro from the Long Beach Naval Shipyard following orders to reactivate the shipyard. The second cause for celebration was re-establishing the Long Beach Naval base to full, active status. As a destroyer broke a ribbon stretched across the entrance of Dry Dock Number 2, the last major event of Navy Day began: resumption of activity at the shipyard. The shipyard had been closed since June, but with the opening approximately 5000-6000 men were expected to be employed at the yard by summer.

On April 15, 1953, families all over America anxiously awaited word about the fate of POWs in Korean War camps. An exchange had been negotiated, but no one knew for sure who would be released or when. The one fact they did have scared them: in order to come home a prisoner had to be sick or wounded. Many wondered if a POW wasn't released if it could be assumed he was OK. Some families were fortunate, having received letters from their loved-ones in a POW camp, others had heard nothing at all and could only hope and pray.

On April 21, 1953, the family of PFC Tibor Rubin was overjoyed to hear he was the first Long Beach soldier released by the Communists. Rubin had been captured November 2, 1950, three months after he had been wounded and returned to duty after recovery in a Tokyo hospital. Rubin, who spent 14 months in a Nazi concentration camp in Hungary during World War II, had only been in the United States 15 months when he joined the Army. He said the Communists urged him to write that he was a Hungarian citizen on prison rosters, but he always wrote "American." His bravery earned the 23-year-old a Purple Heart, but he hoped his captivity by the enemy in Korea was also enough to earn him the right to become an American citizen.

Two days later Long Beach's second POW was released. Marine PFC Joseph P. Britt was coming home. The 19-year-old had been wounded by hand grenade fragments on his legs, chest and arms March 26, 1953, after Chinese overran the Marine outpost on the western front. He was captured eight hours later when he wandered into Chinese trenches. His mother, Helen Horton, heeded what she believed was a Divine message on Easter Sunday (April 5th) reassuring her that her son was still alive. Before that, everyone believed him dead. On Easter Sunday Mrs. Horton believed she heard a voice saying: "Joe is alive. Leave him in God's hands. Stop worrying." After that she knew he was coming home.

Not all families were so fortunate. Thirty-year-old African-American Eugene Pennington was the first Long Beach serviceman whose death in a POW camp was listed by the Communists. The sergeant's wife Elizabeth knew her husband was missing in action but had not known for certain he was in a prisoner of war camp. Her first husband had also been killed in Korea. She was now left with two small sons.

Returning 21-year-old POW Arthur Bowditch was interviewed for a series of articles for the *Press-Telegram* in September 1953. Bowditch had been captured in April 1951 and held prisoner for 28 months. He told that when captured he and fellow prisoners had to walk 350 miles to the camp located, ironically, in a valley called "Peaceful Valley."

One of the POWs had one eye shot out which was hanging down his cheek. The only medical attention he received was his own – he tore off a piece of his clothes and made a patch over his eye. During the march to Peaceful Valley the Reds hid the POWs in tunnels during the day, so American planes couldn't find them, and then marched by night. One morning, as daybreak dawned and they were about to seek shelter, American jets dropped a napalm bomb which singed the prisoners and Korean troops. The prisoners went eight days without food. Some of the men died; weak and starving they were pushed over mountain cliffs while those not able to keep up with the march were clubbed to death while the others watched.

The Peaceful Valley camp had no markings and there was no way that American forces could know that fellow Americans were in the buildings they bombed. One day an American rocket ripped into a room and killed 13 American prisoners. The remaining 400 prisoners were forced to march again to a new camp at Chung Sung.

Bowditch told how he was used by the Reds as a human guinea pig. Doctors cut a hole in his chest, between two ribs, and shoved in what looked like a piece of chicken liver then closed up the incision. Bowditch said they did this to about 100 men, 60 of them died, but the experiment only paralyzed Bowditch from head to foot. His chest became infected and he swelled up like a balloon. Dysentery, malaria, beriberi and tuberculosis also plagued him. Doctors sometimes gave him up to 30 shots a day, but these seemed to help him. While in this disabled state he had to listen hour after hour to Communist doctrine; his captors hoped to convert him to the Red cause.

Bowditch said some of the GIs fell for, or pretended to fall for, the Communist teachings. They received cigarettes, wine and were invited to parties. Some became squealers and told the Chinese about planned prison escapes in return for extra food and medicine. They were hated by the other men and frequently beat up.

There were other returning Long Beach POWs including Sgt. Ralph E. Bishop (1005 E. Hill Street), Lt. Harold A. Steiner (4337 E. 2nd St.), Sgt. Carl E. Gronowicz (5380 Walnut), Clarence L. Anderson (2026 E. 7th St.), Sgt. Robert J. Coffee and Eugene Ramos (822 Truman Boyd Manor).

On July 27, 1953, the Korean conflict would be officially over when the United Nations and North Korea signed an armistice pact. This war had been one of the bloodiest in history and a permanent peace treaty between South Korea and North Korea has never been signed. To this day United States military forces remain in South Korea to discourage a resumption of hostilities between the two Koreas, though peace talks have surfaced once again.

What caused the hostilities? The story begins back in 1895 when the Japanese gained control of the country and made it part of Japan.

When the Allies defeated Japan in World War II the U.S. and Soviet forces moved into Korea. After the war, Soviet troops occupied Korea north of the 38th parallel of north latitude, an imaginary line that cuts the country almost in half. The area south of the 38th parallel was occupied by American troops. In 1947, the United Nations General Assembly declared that a democratic election needed to be held throughout Korea to choose a form of government. The Soviets didn't like this idea and refused to allow elections. However, the people of South Korea elected a national assembly on May 10, 1948, establishing the government of the Republic of Korea. Later that same year the North Korean Communists established the Democratic People's Republic of Korea. Both governments claimed all of Korea, not just their section north or south of the 38th parallel. After the United States removed their troops in 1949, the Communists took action, invading South Korea. In 1953, the war was "officially" at an end but no one was overly optimistic over chances for a permanent peace.

The *USS St. Paul* fired the last shot in the "official" war, lobbing a shell on Red installations just two minutes before the cease fire. She had also been the last major Allied naval vessel to fire on the home islands of Japan at the close of World War II. On November 11, 1953, she sailed into Long Beach; 1700 officers and men swarmed down the gangplanks, glad to be back in America and away from war.

Though the war was over troops were (and are) still stationed in Korea. One famous Navy Reserve officer here to complete a six-week training course (along with 1800 others) at the Long Beach Naval Station was Jon Lindbergh son of Colonel Charles A. Lindbergh.

The second son of the famed "Long Eagle" was born August 16, 1932, two years after his brother Charles Lindbergh Jr. had been kidnapped and found murdered. In appearance Jon, though a few inches shorter than his father, was a virtual carbon-copy of the man who, in 1927, had first flown solo across the Atlantic. Jon was also shy, a quiet man who didn't want all the publicity that seemed to follow him wherever he went. The Stanford University junior just wanted to be treated like any other officer.

Though America was engaged in a new war and former ally Russia had become the country's biggest fear, repercussions from World War II were still being felt. Was Southern California harboring a war criminal? Was Surfside Colony resident Andrija Artukovic guilty of executing 700,000-900,000 Jews, Gypsies, Croats and Serbs in Yugoslavia during World War II? Yugoslavian Premier Tito thought so and charged Artukovic, who had served as puppet Nazi leader in Croatia, with 23 direct murders. Artukovic was also accused of drafting racial laws modeled after Nazi statutes and setting up a network of concentration camps. He was directly charged with the reprisal slaying of civilians in the village of Vrgin Most.

Reporter Drew Pearson, on a nation-wide radio broadcast which aired on April 29, 1951, announced Tito's charges against Artukovic. Bitter, long standing hatred between Serbs and Croats was the underlying factor in the case. Croatia's 7 million population was predominately Catholic, but there were also 1.3 million Serbs in the country that belonged to the Eastern Orthodox Church. Religious differences caused much of the social and political conflict. Forced to come together as one country after World War I, the two groups fought continuously.

Andrija Artukovic was born in Croatia, then part of Austria-Hungary, on November 29, 1899. He studied law and became active in the Croatian separatist movement. In 1934 he was charged, with others, in the assassination of King Alexander of Yugoslavia in Marseilles, but was later acquitted. Afterward he fled Yugoslavia, working with the Nazi party in Germany, Hungary and Austria. When Germany proclaimed the northern portion of Yugoslavia the "Independent State of Croatia" in 1941, Artukovic was named Minister of the Interior.

Artukovic fled to Switzerland after the war and took the name of Alois Anich to escape the Communists. In 1947, he immigrated to Ireland and later came to the United States to work as a bookkeeper in his brother's construction company. As early as 1949 the Immigration and Naturalization Service in Los Angeles knew his true identity, but took no action against him.

Artukovic denied Tito's charges against him and told of saving a train load of 500 Jews on their way to camps in Germany. A Croatian born priest with a parish in Long Beach confirmed Artukovic had nothing to do with the Secret Police and was well thought of by Croatians. Artukovic claimed if he was returned to Yugoslavia he would not get a fair trial and would be executed as had eight other Croatian ministers turned over to Tito by the British government. With Pearson's nationwide announcement, the immigration authorities had no option but to order Artukovic's arrest.

Croatian émigré groups and influential Catholics petitioned for his release. In the anti-Communist fervor of the 1950s he was presented as a victim of the Communists. Though Artukovic was ordered deported, other court decisions threw the deportation question into doubt. The case seesawed back and forth until 1957 when the Supreme Court sent the case back for an immigration rehearing. Commissioners decided Yugoslav affidavits charging Artukovic with murder were unreliable; he could stay in the United States. But Tito didn't give up easily; for almost thirty years Yugoslav officials put pressure on the Justice Department for Artukovic's extradition. Finally in February 1986, Artukovic, labeled in Yugoslavia as the "Butcher of the Balkans," was sent back to Yugoslavia and tried for war crimes.

Throughout the one-month trial Artukovic maintained his innocence. At his trial four specific instances of murder were cited – ordering the deaths of a lawyer and former member of Parliament in 1941; ordering the machine-gun deaths of 450 men women and children because there was no room for them in a concentration camp; ordering the killing of the entire population of a town called Vrgin Most in 1942, and ordering the execution of several hundred prisoners in 1943 by having them driven into an open field where they were machine gunned and then crushed by tanks. Artukovic said he never knew of any killings, and had never been to Vrgin Most.

His words fell on deaf ears. He was convicted of war crimes and sentenced to death. Because of his age and poor health his execution was postponed. Artukovic was to die in a prison hospital in Zagreb on January 16, 1988, at the age of 88. He suffered from Alzheimer's disease, sclerosis, anemia and various heart ailments. To avoid creating a memorial to his memory his body was cremated and his ashes scattered.

Red Scare

Today many look back at the 1950s with nostalgia. It was a time when kids could walk to school and play outside without fear of predators; when Mom could stay home taking care of the family while Dad earned enough money to support them all. But all was not idyllic, there was fear in the air – fear of Communists, UFOs, and the atomic bomb. Adding to this distress was the sighting of mystery submarines.

Between February and April 1950 nine submarines of unknown origin were sighted off the west coast. The Navy pointed out that under international law foreign vessels could freely approach within three miles of the coastline. Within the three-mile limit, however, ships could be stopped and the crew asked to identify themselves. A concerned American public asked why the submarines were here and where were they from.

On April 4, 1950, high Navy officials told the news media they believed the submarines were Russian, but they were also investigating the possibility they could be of Nazi origin. There had been numerous reports at the end of World War II of high Nazis officials fleeing Germany in submarines. It was thought they planned to establish a secret base in some isolated part of the world. Allied intelligence checked these reports thoroughly and found some submarines loaded with equipment for an escape run to Japan. Several were sunk or captured and at least one was found in the Pacific. The Navy believed all were accounted for, but there was always the possibility one or more got away.

Intelligence officers were also interested in the strange disappearance of German-born Theodore Donay, convicted of helping the Nazis during the war. Donay had been sentenced to six and one half years imprisonment in 1943 after failing to report Hans Peter Krug who sought refuge among the Detroit German community after escaping from a Canadian prisoner of war camp in 1942. Donay, a 51-year-old Detroit importer, rented a motorboat and disappeared at sea near Catalina Island at about the same time the Coast Guard sighted an unidentified submarine in Southern California waters.

While civilian authorities searched for Donay's body, naval intelligence investigated the possibility the submarine could have landed someone on the mainland or picked up a person from the sea. In Donay's Catalina hotel room, officers found a suicide note written in German to his brother claiming he couldn't take the harassment he had been subjected to any longer. Many remembered his conviction and prison sentence – he was the first man in American history to be convicted of "misprision (concealment) of treason." A federal court had also taken away his U.S. citizenship, a decision he was in the process of appealing. In the note he said he was going to take his own life.

Avalon officials traced Donay's movements from the time he arrived at the island until he was last seen putting out to sea in a rented motor boat. They reported that after his arrival he checked into the Poly Hotel. Next he visited a hardware store, where he purchased 10 feet of link chain, 10 spools of soldering wire and a pair of pliers. He then rented a boat and ventured out to sea.

Five and one-half hours before the mystery submarine was sighted north of Santa Barbara, the Coast Guard found Donay's motor boat eight miles northeast of Catalina Island. The boat had its running lights on but the ignition turned off. In the boat was a pair of shoes, a dirty, wrinkled gray suit, red scarf, hat and the articles purchased at the hardware store. The newly painted boat had no marks indicating the craft had been beached or brought alongside another boat.

In Donay's room officers found a topcoat, slippers, pajamas, toothbrush and powder, a newly laundered shirt and the suicide note.

They also found receipts which revealed Donay had commercial transactions with Russia totaling $225,000 ($2.5 million in today's money). Could the submarine have been there to pick up Donay, a man worried his appeal to keep his U.S. citizenship would fail and his dealings with the Russians unearthed?

When a body was discovered on April 8, 1950, wrapped in chain a half mile off Corona del Mar, many thought it was Donay. The death was ruled a suicide, but the body was that of Frederick Parsons, a 68-year-old retired merchant seaman. Donay was never found. On May 5, 1950, the Sixth U.S. Circuit Court of Appeals upheld a federal court decision revoking Donay's U.S. citizenship. The Korean and Cold wars, plus mystery submarines off the coast were making Americans nervous. Many felt Communism was to blame, and something had to be done about it. On September 1, 1950, all Communists in unincorporated areas of Los Angeles County were required to register at sheriff's offices throughout the county. Failure to do so would result in six months in jail, a $500 fine, or both. This unprecedented county ordinance did maintain confidentiality to a point. Names of those who registered would not be made public, but it would keep registrants from owning weapons or being appointed to any of the county's civilian defense positions. Later, historians would describe this period as the "Second Red Scare," also known as McCarthyism, which lasted from approximately 1947 to 1956 (the "First Red Scare" was from 1917-1920 following the start of the Russian Revolution). Wisconsin Senator Joseph McCarthy is credited with starting the "fear" by alleging that numerous Communists and Soviet spies had infiltrated government institutions, colleges, the film industry and elsewhere.

What was the definition of a Communist? According to the county it was anyone who advocated the overthrow of the government by force or violence, encouraged illegal interference which would hamper production of materials for military or civilian defense purposes, or would impose minority rule of totalitarian dictatorship on the majority. The county wasn't the only one passing laws, the

McCarran Internal Security Act of 1950 provided for the possible internment of Communists during a national emergency.

The county ordinance did not apply to incorporated cities – it was up to each municipality in Los Angeles County to decide how they wanted to handle the issue.

On August 29, 1950, Long Beach City Prosecutor Kenneth E. Sutherland presented a proposed ordinance to the Long Beach City Council which would require all Communists in the city to register or suffer a $500 fine or six months in jail or both. He told the council there were organized Communist groups in Long Beach. He was worried about possible sabotage at the harbor and at local businesses. Police Chief William Dovey didn't feel Long Beach needed a special ordinance. He had the county list of known Communists. Congress was also considering a bill which would outlaw the Communist Party in the United States. Dovey felt this was sufficient. But the "Red Scare" was in the air. The City Council unanimously approved an ordinance requiring registration of all Communists residing in Long Beach and also of all Communists passing through the city.

Though the American Civil Liberties Union went to court charging the county and Long Beach ordinances violated both federal and state constitutions, Long Beach residents didn't care. They were well aware of the "Red Menace" having just read excerpts from Fulton Oursler's new book *Why I Know There is a God*, in the *Press-Telegram* newspaper. In the book Oursler told the world that civilization had to choose between Christ and Communism. All Long Beach folk knew who they would choose.

Also in the press, and fresh in everyone's minds, were the Alger Hiss case and the Communist conspiracy to take over America. Suspicion was everywhere. Following Truman's Executive Order 9835 in 1947, which required that all federal civil service employees be screened for loyalty, California enacted its own loyalty oath for state and local employees.

When all 3219 Long Beach city employees were asked to take the state mandated oath in October 1950, all but one agreed; they didn't want their friends and neighbors to think they were disloyal to America. They also didn't want to lose their jobs. Rules for taking the oath were very explicit. Each employee had to repeat the oath, word for word. Anyone refusing to take the oath would be fired and the penalty for lying was 14 years imprisonment. One Long Beach crossing guard refused to take the oath. This was not because he was a Communist but because of religious scruples. He resigned from his job.

In May 1954, Mrs. Helen Wood Birnie, a Lakewood mother of four told the *Press-Telegram*, in a series of articles, what it was like to be a Communist.

For three years, Mrs. Birnie was not only a Communist but a Communist party organizer as well. Those years were behind her now, she told a reporter, and she had become one of Communism's severest critics. In March 1953, she testified before the House Un-American Activities Committee speaking of the threat of Communism in this country. She was now working for the Christian Anti-Communism Crusade and spoke throughout the U.S. on the dangers of Communism.

Helen Birnie told *Press-Telegram* reporter Ben Zinser about joining the Communist party in Great Falls, Montana, in 1932. Soon afterwards she received a letter from the Central Committee in New York telling her that due to the lack of leadership in the Mountain States District she had been appointed to the office of district organizer – quite an accomplishment for a 21-year-old. She took her appointment seriously. Whenever a tough fight was being waged on the labor front she was there. If a race riot was imminent she would be in the middle of it. Why did she join the party? It wasn't because of Marx or political theory, she said, it was because she was angry about her maladjusted childhood. She became a bitter enemy of the accepted order of things – she became a Communist.

Never paid a penny for her work, Helen Birnie lived with other Communists while she worked with the International Labor Defense, a Communist-front organization. In Omaha, Nebraska, where she had her headquarters, she lived with an aged Negro couple who were friendly to the party because it talked so much about making things easier for their race. The house was lighted by kerosene because the couple couldn't afford to pay for gas. Sometimes there was only one meal a day. One woman provided Helen with second-hand clothes. It was a faithful Negro group – all non-party members – who kept her going financially.

Her day started at 4 a.m. She would head to Omaha's packing house district to hand out leaflets to the arriving workers. She then headed to the Communist district office, to discuss strategy on how to infiltrate labor and agriculture unions. Afternoons and evenings were spent picketing or holding meetings preaching Communist doctrines. She also hired lawyers to defend labor organizers who were arrested. In addition, she had to study a number of Communist periodicals and then answer questions showing she had indeed studied them. In three years' time she hitchhiked more than 30,000 miles, through raging blizzards, often with only 15 cents in her pocket, to reach other Communist centers in the Mountain State District. All her ties with former friends were severed, only the party was important to her.

In Iowa she became disenchanted with the Communist party and realized she was being used. Her African-American friends pleaded with Helen to help an 18-year-old Negro, the only wage earner in a family of eight, who was being held for first-degree murder. All evidence pointed to his not being guilty but the Communist Section Committee of Iowa instructed her to leave the case alone. This infuriated Helen. She put two and two together and realized there were only 6000 African-Americans in Des Moines at the time and not all were voters. The party didn't consider this number important enough to help. Helen disobeyed the orders and worked on the case, eventually ending up getting the young man a bench parole. The Section Committee charged her with insubordination and unbecoming conduct. Enraged, she tore up her party book. When they tried to get her to reconsider her membership, she refused. She turned to God instead.

Helen Birnie told reporter Zinser that until she returned to God she did not become either a useful citizen or a willing one. As a Christian, she warned of the Communist threat of today. The organization had changed since Helen was an organizer for three years in the 1930s; then she made no secret of the fact she was a Communist, but that was not the case for party members today. Currently (in 1954) there were from 27,000 to 30,000 Communists in the United States, according to FBI director J. Edgar Hoover. For those that thought this too small a number to do any damage, Helen Birnie had this to say:

Just remember this: One rotten apple can spoil the entire barrel. That's not trite. That's true. It's a good picture of what a Communist cell can do in an area or organization in dealing with the Communist party; we are confronted with persons skilled in espionage, sabotage and revolution. Communists are meticulous. They are sternly disciplined. They are dedicated. They will go to any lengths to accomplish their objectives. (Press-Telegram5/23/1954)

Helen Birney was a member of the Christian Anti-Communism Crusade, founded in Iowa in 1953, by Dr. Fred Schwarz. Schwarz moved the Crusade's operations to Long Beach in 1960, where the headquarters remained until Dr. Schwarz' retirement in 1998. Schwarz, an Australian born Christian evangelist, became concerned about the Communist states, particularly the Soviet Union. He made an extensive study of leading Communist theorists, Marx, Engels and Lenin, which led him to believe it was a very bad idea that led to tyranny, misery and the deaths of millions. Schwarz opposed Communism not for political or economic reasons, but because of its attitude to God and man. He felt compelled to take action. He closed his medical practice and moved to the United States in the early 1950s where he found an audience ready to listen to his methodical analysis and the dangers that Communism presented.

In the book *Patriotism or Paranoia?*, author Robert Sellen described Schwarz' manner as a mixture of London music hall and fundamentalist preacher; his Australian accent and humorous opening remarks were blended with emotionalism. Schwarz' amazing memory allowed him to quote verbatim, for hours, the political works of Lenin and others. With respectable sponsors ranging from churches to United States Senators, he gave lectures, showed films and sold books. Not political, like the John Birch Society, the Christian Anti-Communism Crusade was forbidden, under crusade policy, to offer political legislative action; instead the crusade preached that citizens needed to turn to God with renewed dedication to assure victory over Communism.

Shortly after relocating to Long Beach, Schwarz told the *Los Angeles Times* that Communism was making considerable progress in America as expressed with the then popular slogan used by the young – "better Red than dead." He believed the fundamental problem was that 99% of the "servants" of Communism didn't know they were serving. During the UC Berkley demonstrations in 1965 Schwarz declared they were the result of Communist advances. "The university campus has always served as the best Communist recruiting ground," Schwarz said. It was on college campuses that Communists were gaining ground. To combat this intrusion into American society Schwarz instituted his own "School of Anti-Communism" to fight this ignorance.

The five day sessions, held throughout the U.S., ran from 8:30 a.m. to 9:30 p.m. The *Los Angeles Times* reported the August 28-September 1, 1961 school, held in the 16,000 seat Los Angeles Memorial Sports Arena, was filled to capacity. The four evening sessions, featuring nationally known speakers, were broadcast on television station KTTV (11) live, preempting normal prime time programs. It was sponsored by Richfield Oil Company as a public service. Three million television viewers watched nightly. The goal of the program was to familiarize Americans with the subject of Communism in order to combat the growing, subversive threat to our way of life.

Schwarz' rhetoric reached celebrities such as Pat Boone, Roy Rogers, Jimmy Stewart, George Murphy, John Wayne and Ronald Reagan. At the 1961 Los Angeles school Ronald Reagan asserted that the trend to a welfare state and more centralized government in America was as dangerous as Communism. Years later when

Reagan became president he engaged several of Schwartz' former Anti-Communism School students as speechwriters. Their work included the famous "Evil Empire" speech, which heralded a new era in U.S. political engagement with the Soviet Union. When asked what he thought about the John Birch Society, another anti-communist organization, Schwarz said he had never met Robert Welch, head of the group. He said he was not referring specifically to the John Birch Society, but he was worried that concern without knowledge led to fanaticism. That was why he started his schools. In addition to his schools, Schwarz was drawing turn-away crowds to his anti-subversive talks in stadiums nationwide. He travelled a lot, promoting his newsletter and lecturing on the evils of Communism. His twice monthly newsletter, which had a circulation of 36,000 in 1976, was also sent unsolicited to 3,000 colleges and 4,000 news media organizations. He also made his way regularly on to television in California, sponsored by the Schick Safety Razor Corporation and the Technicolor Corporation.

Interviewed by *Press-Telegram* reporter Brad Altman in 1976, Altman pointed out that Schwarz had earned a good income since founding the crusade. His yearly salary in 1976 was $25,000 ($108,000 in 2017 dollars). In 1975, the nonprofit organization grossed $547,161 ($2,490,000 in 2017). Schwarz agreed with the figures, but added that all royalties from his book sales went to the crusade. When Brad Altman asked him about the status of Communism in the United States, Schwarz replied: "the Communists will not take over by winning at the ballot box or by the classic scenario of an internal workers revolution or by victory in a nuclear war. Surrender will come through external encirclement plus internal demoralization leading to progressive surrender." (*Independent 9/12/1976*).

Frederick Charles Schwarz, who was at odds with many in the liberal left through the 1960s and 1970s, died at age 96 in Camden, Australia, on January 24, 2009.

It seemed that Helen Birnie was right about Communists going to any lengths to accomplish their objectives. On November 12, 1953, the *Long Beach Press-Telegram* had flashed an alarming headline: "Red Agents Seized in L.B. Harbor Area." The Coast Guard disclosed that a group of "nationally known Communist agents" had apparently infiltrated a heavily guarded security area at the harbor and were caught near a ship loaded with "highly secret cargo."

The potential saboteurs were not named but the port captain said a check of files in government intelligence and law enforcement agencies definitely established that five of the nine men were known Communist agents. All the men were immediately ejected from the security area and released. The Coast Guard explained they would prefer to keep the men in the open where the FBI could keep their eyes on them rather than in jail. The Coast Guard went on to state that they frequently had trouble with known Communists at the port, but this case was "special" because of the top priority defense cargo aboard the ship in question.

Who were these men who had been caught? They could be your next door neighbor or even one of the speakers at the long-standing "University by the Sea" on the Rainbow Pier. Also known as the "Spit and Argue Club," the famous institution had been part of Long Beach since 1935. Here people talked about whatever they wanted and argued with people of the opposite viewpoint for hours on end.

In February 1953 the American Legion declared that Long Beach's renowned "University by the Sea" was being used to preach Communist doctrine. It wouldn't be very nice for a father who lost a boy in Korea hear the Commies talk against the government," one man told the *Press-Telegram*. Others agreed, but said they doubted whether any of the speakers in question were actually card-carrying Communists, but many were Communist sympathizers. The Legion asked the Recreation Commission to abolish the club's platform on the pier. Instead the commission ordered increased supervision of the club with Recreation Department and Police Department staff patrolling the area. They also suggested the Legion provide speakers to preach patriotic themes.

Little did the Recreation Commission realize that the American Legion and the alleged Communist sympathizers would come to actual blows. On December 22, 1953, 68-year-old Patrick Fitzpatrick was convicted on battery charges after he admitted slugging a "University by the Sea" opponent. The former CIO labor leader was charged with socking Leslie M. Abercrombie, 55, vice chairman of the Anti-Communist Society of Los Angeles, after both men had finished speaking from the University's rostrum. Fitzpatrick testified that Abercrombie referred to himself as an "undercover man for the FBI." Fitzpatrick then offered Abercrombie $5 to prove it. Abercrombie responded with "I know your dirty Communist line." Fitzpatrick said he was basically a peaceful man but when Abercrombie started shaking his finger at him he had had enough. He hit him on the nose and gave him an uppercut to the jaw.

A standing room crowd of 125 spectators, crammed into the courtroom, were impressed by the theatrics, but the performance failed to move the judge. Patrick W. Fitzpatrick was found guilty of battery. However, his 10-day jail term and $50 fine was suspended. Instead he was granted a year's probation on condition he refrained from heckling or otherwise interrupting speakers at the Spit and Argue Club.

Inflammatory mail dealing with local, state and national issues hit town in 1958. Pamphlets from Box 27103 in Hollywood were received by the Long Beach City Council, civic leaders and citizens at large whenever controversial issues were under discussion. When the City Council was considering establishing a mental health service, Box 27103 sent out eight pages of arguments stating that a mental health program meant Communist domination because it changed people's attitudes. When fluoridation of water to prevent tooth decay was being considered by voters, Box 27103 got busy again. It sent out a piece of paper known as the Goff affidavit which said in part:

While a member of the Communist party I attended a Communist underground training school...We discussed thoroughly the fluoridation of water supplies and how we were using it in Russia as a tranquilizer in prison camps. The leaders of our school felt that if it could be introduced into the American water supply it would bring about lethargy and keep the public docile during the encroachment of Communism. (Press-Telegram 5/11/1958)

The missive was successful in defeating water fluoridation in Long Beach for many years. The fluoridation measure was finally approved in 1970, and implemented on June 22, 1971.

Who was behind P.O. Box 27103? Mrs. Phyllis M. Seldon, a gray-haired woman, living in a tiny apartment in Los Angeles had signed for the box. She was a member of the Committee for the Preservation of the Constitution who also used P.O. Box 27103 as its mailing address. Mrs. Seldon said the Committee for the Preservation of the Constitution had nothing to do with the campaign against mental health programs – that was her own project. She said she and the Committee had no funds, but that "friends" were footing the bill.

The Atomic Age

From July 20-29, 1951, people from all over the Southland traveled to Long Beach's Veteran's Stadium to learn more about atomic energy. One of the major attractions was the model atom smasher and model atomic pile which was designed to educate the public as to the uses and origin of atomic energy. A demonstration of how a family could survive under an atomic attack was also part of the exposition. Earlier that month the Federal Civil Defense Administration (FCDA) had urged every household in America to prepare for a nuclear war.

Ever since the end of World War II Americans were afraid of the nuclear capabilities of the Russian Communists. Their fear was well founded when the Soviets launched their first atmospheric nuclear test, in Semipalatinsk, Kazakhstan, in August 1949. Soon Long Beach residents were issued steps to take in case of an atom-bomb attack:

- *First indication of an atomic burst will be a sudden burst of light. If possible, don't look at the light. Try to cover all exposed parts of the body.*
- *If you are in the open when the sudden light comes, drop instantly to the ground and curl up to cover bare arms and hands, neck and face with clothing. The curled-up position should be held for at least 10 seconds with your back to the light before standing up.*
- *If you are in the street and some sort of protection such as a doorway, a corner, or a tree is no more than a step or two away, you may take shelter there with your back to the light and in a crouched position.*

- *Wait at least 10 seconds before you stand up. No attempt should be made to reach a shelter even if it is several steps off.*
- *The radioactivity of the atomic bomb while serious has been exaggerated. Actually, it causes less casualties than blast or heat. Since radioactivity may linger after an explosion, don't be in too much of a hurry to leave your home or shelter after a raid. (Press-Telegram 9/15/1950)*

Local residents were often reminded of the "bomb" when windows rattled and a brilliant flash was seen in the east. The flash, which resembled sudden dawn lighting up the mountains, was just another atom bomb being tested in the desert around Las Vegas.

In August 1945, the United States dropped nuclear devices over Hiroshima and Nagasaki, hastening the Japanese surrender that ended World War II. A new era in history had begun – the Atomic Age. In 1946, Congress created the Atomic Energy Commission (AEC) to oversee nuclear development. Fearing a threat from the Soviet nuclear program the AEC authorized nuclear weapons tests in the South Pacific, and then later decided the Nevada desert would be less vulnerable to attack. In December 1950, the commission recommended setting up a permanent proving ground on a piece of the old Las Vegas Bombing and Gunnery Range. President Truman agreed and the first atmospheric detonation at Frenchman Flat, part of the Nevada Test Site, took place one month later.

Before the Nevada Test Site was a nuclear bombing range it had been an animal sanctuary. In the 1930s, the Department of the Interior made the region a wildlife reservation. Centuries earlier, Native Americans lived in the caves in the mountains. In the mid-1800s, settlers built silver and copper mining camps, providing names such as Skull Mountain, Indian Springs, and Jackass Flats. But by 1942 America had entered World War II, and the entire region was withdrawn from public access for War Department use. After the war the area was no longer needed by the military, but the Army hung on to the land rights for possible future use. That future became clear when 1,350 acres was parceled off and called the Nevada Test Site.

On January 27, 1951, at 5:45 a.m., an Air Force B-50D bomber dropped the first atomic bomb on U.S. soil – a dry lakebed called Frenchman Flat, inside the Nevada Test Site. More tests were held in subsequent days. The February 2nd blast was seen 425 miles away in San Francisco despite an intervening 14,000 foot range of mountains. It was sighted in Long Beach at 5:55 a.m. Al Seate was at Junipero and Magnolia talking to some of his newspaper carriers when the flash occurred. He said a complete outline of the mountains was exposed. Travis Westerman in North Long Beach described an orange colored flash which lasted a couple of seconds, while Lee Williams thought it looked like a big flash bulb with a greenish tinge. Las Vegas residents were worried when they saw a long pencil-like tan cloud which hung in the sky northeast of the city above 11,000 feet. The cloud remained for 2 hours. It caused the AEC to depart from its usual one paragraph statement that another test had been held. Instead they announced that there was no indication of radiological hazards to animals, humans, or the water supply. This was the first time the AEC had mentioned water supply, and it made some people nervous. That same day children in Rochester, New York, Chicago and Cincinnati played in "atomic snow." Radioactive particles from the explosion had mixed with the ice in the atmosphere. The government assured citizens this radioactive snow held no danger.

George Flowers, the *Press-Telegram* City Editor, was one of 20 press representatives allowed to witness an atomic blast in March 1953. For the first time television cameras were allowed into the target area to bring viewers a first-hand account of the explosion and its aftermath. Flowers brought local readers a vivid description of his experience:

We stood to watch. Before us was the greatest, most angry work of art ever created by man. A boiling, churning, raging cloud was a mass of changing bright colors. There were purples, reds, yellows and oranges in a display that was only magnificent. It was as though a great artist had painted a picture of violent anger on an ever changing screen. Upward boiled the cloud and its orange hues faded swiftly...Officers said the hydrogen was now burning out. You will never see anything more beautiful. (Press-Telegram 3/17/1953)

People throughout America rushed to any nearby television to get a glimpse of this awesome spectacle. It was frightening to think a thing so beautiful could cause so much destruction, but they were not afraid that something could go wrong, after all this was America. All they worried about was that without the tests the Russians held the upper hand. It was terrifying to many when Civil Defense Authorities said they believed the Long Beach/Los Angeles harbor would be number 3 on a hit list if the Russians did start a nuclear war.

On the same day Flowers published his first-hand report, the *Press-Telegram* printed a map showing the area that would be affected if a bomb was dropped on Long Beach City Hall at Pacific and Broadway. It showed that heavy damage would extend to about Hill Street, and to the east it would go beyond Cherry Avenue. To the west the entire harbor and Navy base would be destroyed. To this unsettling news was added an unknown factor – Russia would soon have a new head of state. Stalin had died March 6, 1953; who knew what the next Russian leader would do.

With hindsight it's now coming out that the atomic bomb tests were more dangerous than the Russians. For 41 years the United States conducted 928 nuclear tests, with 1,021 total detonations. Most were underground, but 100 tests were atmospheric, or out in the open. The last detonation was in September 1992. But in the early years of nuclear testing Americans had no real fear of radiation, but years later the truth about the dangers of atomic bomb fallout caused the aging baby boom generation to take a hard look at their childhoods, their health, and what they might have been exposed to.

In the summer of 1997 a National Cancer Institute (NCI) report was issued stating people as far away as the East Coast may have been exposed to as much radiation fallout from the nuclear tests in the 1950s as residents directly downwind from the Nevada blasts.

This exposure to radioactive iodine raised the possibility that 10,000 to 75,000 children at the time would develop thyroid cancer. The report stated that young children's exposures may have been 10 times the average in the worst hot spots, mostly because they drank contaminated milk. Everyone in the 48 contiguous states between 1951 and 1958 received some fallout from the 90 nuclear bomb tests in Nevada, the NCI study found, and anyone worried about fallout exposure during childhood was advised to get a thyroid examination. Fortunately thyroid cancer is a slow-growing, highly curable, cancer with a five-year survival rate of 95 percent.

When mysterious objects began to fall from the sky, many believed they were debris from atomic bombs. In 1954, the "pock-marked windshield caper" was in the news when pitted windows appeared suddenly throughout the west. In Washington State, residents had suffered through two days of crescent-shaped scars appearing in their windshields. This "epidemic" later hit Oregon and Long Beach.

The pock-marking started in Long Beach in March 1954. Robert Krieder, Otis Ritchie and J.D. Cross each reported pock-marks and ash on their vehicles. It seemed each pock-mark had a small brown area in the middle which spread out like spider webs. Amazingly the pits seemed to grow in size. Leah Elkins saw tiny cracks spread rapidly over the rear window of her 1950 model car while she was watching from several feet away. The pitted window just suddenly "happened" while the car was parked in a lot on Ocean Boulevard and Long Beach Boulevard. Could it have been a malfunction in the glass, or something caused by H-bombs? "Experts" later explained that the pitting was the result of normal driving conditions in which small objects struck the windshield. Ash from a nuclear bomb was definitely not the cause. However, not all were sure the answer was an honest one.

Flying ash continued to hit Long Beach. On March 22, 1954, the Fitzgerald family of 3617 E. Eighth Street observed ash in the sky.

They could see big chunks larger than a baseball and higher than a eucalyptus tree floating above them. They knew the ashes weren't ordinary. Nobody in the neighborhood had an incinerator and it was raining at the time. Two other families reported similar sightings. Though nuclear tests were held in March and April of 1954, they were so far away in the Bikini Atoll that scientists doubted any ash could have travelled as far as the west coast. No one could say where the ashes which fell that March day in Long Beach came from.

Mystery objects continued to fall from the sky in 1954. Arthur Anakun was watering his lawn at 3140 Mariquita Street in September 1954 when a stone hit his palm tree then plopped to the ground beside him. When he picked it up it was so hot he had to drop it, but having his hose nearby, Anakin cooled the object off, then looked at it with a magnifying glass. He scraped off about an eighth-inch hard outer shell, revealing a smooth, amber stone with patches of light blue with streaks of gold. Was it a meteorite? A piece of an atomic bomb? Nobody seemed to know.

Authorities were also puzzled when 50 chunks of ice, some as heavy as 150 pounds, fell like bombs for two minutes on the 1400 and 1500 blocks of American Avenue in June 1953. Two autos were dented, but fortunately no one was injured. The blocks, as much as three or four feet long, were variously described as ice formed by an atomic blast, material de-iced by a plane flying overhead or ice which somehow fell out of a plane transporting perishables. The Civil Aeronautics Authority said the ice was definitely the type that formed on the surfaces of high-flying planes and it was possible it came from an Air Force B-36 Continental bomber allegedly flying overhead about the same time. Another Air Force official, Lt. Col. Paul Light said it was extremely doubtful that ice of such enormous size could form on the wings of even the largest planes. The theory that it might have fallen from a cargo plane was also discounted since the only local cargo plane which might have dumped the ice left for Mexico early in the morning and had not returned. The associate director of the Griffith Observatory said he could not imagine such a large amount of ice forming in the atmosphere, and only minute particles of ice would come from an atomic bomb. What was it?

On June 19, 1965, Jack and Treva Adair of 1612 E. 3rd St. were awakened by a loud noise. Jack, a retired music teacher, thought someone had hit the house with a baseball bat. He went out to see if someone was beside the house, but saw no one and heard no footsteps. The following morning he found his window screen slashed and loosened. On the hardwood window sill was a jagged gouge, about a half-inch long. He then found another gouge, indicating that whatever hit there had rebounded. On the ground beside the house Adair found a peculiar object, the one that had crashed into his house. The three-inch long by two-inch wide object looked like but didn't seem to be a rock, or an asphalt hunk. It rather defied description. It weighed about six or seven ounces, was porous but hard and contained what appeared to be sparkling bits of silica. It also had what seemed to be a partial mud-like coating of some kind. It was rough and irregular, except for one side, which was flat. Neighbors also heard the noise when it smashed into the window sill with enough force to imbed the enamel coating into the wood of the sill.

Curious, Adair took it to a nearby fire station that put it under a Geiger counter. It was slightly radioactive What was it? A meteorite or something from the exhaust of a jet plane? No one seemed to know so Adair sent the object to UCLA for analysis. It turned out to be asphalt and probably had been part of a highway or an airport runway. Speculation was the asphalt had been wedged in the tread of an airplane tire and eventually came loose. In any case it was dangerous. Ellen Kiewiet, who also had been exposed to another case of falling asphalt, reported it came down quickly and grazed the face of her 4-year-old daughter. The family was fortunate it hadn't hit little Marean full face.

Marean wasn't the only child to escape serious injury by falling objects. On November 15, 1965, a 50-pound object fell from the atmosphere narrowly missing children who were on their way to school. In this instance, police knew what the object was – a Navy fighter plane's tow target. The target, painted red with a spear-like projection and round ball the size of a bowling ball sheared off branches from a eucalyptus tree as it fell in front of the W. R. Jones home at 2426 Adriatic about 8:45 in the morning. Police and firemen cordoned off the immediate area while a demolition team from the U.S. Naval Weapons Station at Seal Beach extricated the object which protruded about two feet from the ground. Several Navy spokesmen were surprised a tow target would have been over a populated area. Interestingly, a check of naval air stations throughout the area failed to trace the plane.

A bolt from the blue – a 1/1/2 inch long, quarter-inch thick, case hardened steel bolt hit the Sam Blevins' home at 5156 Parkcrest on December 21, 1965. The still warm bolt didn't come from Santa's sled on a test run but from a twin-engine plane which Mrs. Blevins remembered seeing flying overhead. Upon investigation the FAA said it appeared to be the bolt from a slip joint on an airplane exhaust system.

Other things were falling from the sky including a Russian space rocket that streaked over Long Beach on February 15, 1967. The brilliant aerial show began at 8:30 p.m. and was variously identified as a meteor, an airplane on fire, a rocket, and a flying saucer. But the final word came from the North American Air Defense Command in Colorado Springs. Officials of the command said the object was the rocket of a Russian satellite launched on February 8, 1967. Fortunately the decaying rocket broke up and fell into the ocean rather than over Long Beach homes.

In July 1951 the Federal Civil Defense Administration (FCDA) urged every household in America to prepare an emergency first-aid kit and store it in a bomb-shelter area. Twelve million pamphlets listed the 20 items to go into each kit, and the purpose of each item. They included: antiseptic solution, aromatic spirits of ammonia, table salt, baking soda, four triangular bandages, two large bath towels, two small bath towels, one bed sheet, two medium first-aid dressings, two small first-aid dressings, 25 to 50 paper drinking cups, eye drops, flashlight, 15 safety pins, three single-edge razor blades, toilet soap, 12 plastic or wooden splints, 12 wooden tongue blades, 100 water purification tablets and a set of plastic or metal measuring spoons. Experts said the whole kit shouldn't cost more than $2 or $3. It was also advised to have three days' supply of food and water in closed containers for each family member since consumption of food or water exposed to atomic radiation would be fatal.

In August 1951, Ray D. Spencer resigned as chief of the nation's bomb shelter program after the House turned down a $250,000,000 shelter construction program. Spencer told the press that virtually all the 31 million Americans in "critical target" areas of 54 cities were so poorly protected against atomic bombs they would not survive a large scale attack. Also cut from the budget was civil defense funding. President Truman had requested $535,000,000 for civil defense, instead receiving approval for only $65,255,000.

Part of the Federal Civil Defense funds that year went towards an atom age game featuring Bert the Turtle, a cartoon character with a built-in bomb shelter. Bert was used to teach children what to do if enemy A-bombs hit. Bert was selected, the FCDA said, because he "ducks and covers by instinct at the threat of danger, pulling in his head and completely shielding himself with his shell." Bert's tricks were shown in a 16-page illustrated booklet – *Duck and Cover.*

Long Beach, like many other American cities, began designating bomb shelters in public buildings with whatever civil defense funds they had available. By September 1951, eight downtown buildings had been chosen as shelters – the basements of City Hall, Veterans Memorial building, Public Utilities building, Montgomery Ward, Wise building, Press-Telegram building, Independent building and the city garage. The FCDA told Americans if they were caught in a direct target of a bomb they would probably never know what hit them. But outside that two-mile range individuals would stand a good chance of survival if they found their way into a shelter.

There were some bomb shelters in Long Beach constructed during World War II, such as the one wedged in between the front steps of the Nu-Pike Plunge at 201 W. Pike. But it would not help in surviving a nuclear bomb. Built in 1940 of foot-thick reinforced concrete, the bomb shelter later became home to a palm reading concession, then a first-aid station, and finally a hot-dog stand before it was torn down in January 1958.

What to do after an attack? The government funded booklet stated: remain calm. Follow instructions of civil defense workers. Keep radio on to receive authorized instructions. Do not use your car or telephone except in cases of extreme emergency for cars could block roads needed by rescue workers and needless use of phones tied up essential communications. If you were within a contaminated area: remain in your home or shelter until advised by radio or civil defense workers that it was safe to leave. Remove garments and bathe, using plenty of strong soap. Do not consume food or water or use any objects which may have been exposed to radioactive contamination. However, it would be safe to use food from tight containers and water that had been stoppered or in other closed vessels.

Long Beach resident Maurice Cohn wasn't taking any chances with his family. In January 1951 Cohn took out a permit for an underground bomb shelter at his property at 1480 Marshall Place. The shelter designed by Engineer Paul J. Proust reportedly would withstand a pressure of 2100 pounds per square foot. The 6 foot wide, 14 foot long, 11 foot deep structure was built of reinforced concrete. Sunset Fence and Patio Company (3626 Long Beach Blvd.), contractors for Cohn's shelter, advertised they would "build for you a scientifically engineered sub-surface bomb shelter in your back yard. Built according to rigid specifications – Designed by a licensed engineer. FHA terms. 10% down – 30 months to pay." Costs of shelters could run from $300 to $1000.

Some, like Long Beach police officer Robert Hacker, built their own shelters. Hacker, who resided at 2930 Delta Avenue, used 750 feet of steel reinforcing rod and more than 18 cubic yards of concrete.

The family's shelter was 10 feet long, 7 feet wide and 6 feet 10 inches high, walls were 14 inches thick and equipped with air vents, a small ice box and electric lights. If you weren't sure how to build a shelter *Your bomb shelter plan book,* published in Long Beach was hot off the press. The 40 pages of "authoritative information," including plans of six engineered shelters, could be had for only $1.

Long Beach's first apartment house with a built-in bomb shelter was constructed on the northeast corner of Appleton and Hermosa Streets in 1953. R.A. Hoffa and Associates were the owners and Don Muntz the architect. The "Hermosa" an eight apartment, two bedroom own-your-own stucco and frame building had an underground concrete 15x25 foot bomb shelter. Located below the garage, the shelter was large enough to seat 20 people in an emergency. In addition, the bomb shelter had a steel door protected by a concrete canopy with steel benches for seating. There were also cabinets in which to hold food, water, medical supplies and other necessities. By placing the laundry room over the shelter the cost was reduced. The Hermosa apartments were priced from $9950. Hoffa had this to say:

With the recent explosions of atomic energy in Nevada and examinations into the extent of damage to residential buildings and injury to occupants, the time has come to start thinking about protection to persons and property. With this thought in mind our firm decided to carry some measure of safety to the public and this resulted in the program we've now launched in Long Beach." (Press-Telegram 7/26/1953)

By 1955 bomb shelters had become a real estate selling point. They were included in the listing along with the usual swimming pool, patio, wine cellar, and servant quarters. Moore Realty advertised "Free Bomb Shelter. You can have a free bomb shelter or convert this to a swimming pool which is included in this 4 bedroom, 2 bath home for only $79.87/ month." *(Ind. Press-Telegram 8/14/1955)*

Bomb shelters were big business. In February 1958 the Hercules Bomb Shelter Company of 5529 E. Spring, held a drawing for a free bomb shelter to be installed at no additional charge. Their full page ad in the February 13, 1958 *Press-Telegram* stated:

Here are some of the facts we must learn to live with in what President Eisenhower has called "an age of peril."

1. *Atomic and hydrogen bombs do exist as deliverable weapons of war. The Russians are known beyond any doubt to possess a growing stockpile of such weapons.*
2. *No absolute military defense exists today or is likely to exist in the foreseeable future. A determined aggressor could deliver atomic or hydrogen bombs in our cities, should he decide to attack our country.*
3. *If the bomb does come your way seek the best available shelter. An ordinary frame house will offer some protection. It may cut radiation danger by about one-half. Get on the floor, away from doors and windows, or preferably go to a location at the center of the house. A basement shelter will offer even more protection. The radiation danger there might be one-tenth as bad. An underground shelter with 3 feet of earth above it will give you almost complete protection if it is equipped with a door and an air filter.*

Underground bomb shelters were recommended, but you could also survive in your own home, as an April 1955 experiment, the first of its kind anywhere, according to the *Press-Telegram*, hoped to prove.

The Frank George family of 5650 E. 23rd Street in the Los Altos district volunteered. Calling their project "Operation Guinea Pig," it was backed by civilian defense officials and the *Press-Telegram*. Stella George, a freelance writer would write a daily report and describe how the family of four coped during three days and nights, virtual prisoners in their own home, while they tested living conditions following a nuclear bomb attack. Their entire food supply would consist of $5.90 worth of rations listed in the official government survival food kit. The family of four kit recommended three large cans of fruit juice, two small cans of meat, four cans of vegetables, one can of soup and three cans of fruit, together with crackers, dry cereal and beverages. In addition, the George family would be living without electric lights, running water and gas.

The scenario was as follows: Stella George preparing dinner at 6 p.m. when word of the alert comes over the television. Everyone springs into action – daughters Diane and Vicki closing windows and drawing blinds while their mother turns off the kitchen appliances, and their dad brings in the pets from outside and locks the doors. They then settle down to the long, three-day test. The nuclear bomb, it is assumed, falls 20 or 30 miles away. The Georges must stay indoors because of radioactivity. For the first eight hours they will stay, somewhat cramped, in the hallway. Then they will use the remainder of the house. Cooking will be done on a gasoline camping stove and light will come from a lantern.

The experiment began the evening of April 12, 1955. Boredom and trying to explain to 6-year-old Vicki why she couldn't go outside or watch television were the major problems. Keeping the pets inside was also difficult; their well-trained dog finally wetted the floor after 40 hours of confinement, looking very guilty. Summing up their three day "adventure" Stella George wrote that having no running water presented the greatest physical problem. She recommended that mustard be added to the list to spice up the food, and small cans of milk be substituted for fruit juices. More meat, soup and coffee were definitely needed because the family was always hungry – Stella and George lost 4 pounds during the test, daughter Vicki 3 pounds, and 12-year-old Diane 2 pounds. Stella said the second day seemed to be the lowest ebb, and more food would have helped with the ennui. She felt that a three-day supply of pet food and an inexpensive first aid kit for pets should also be in a family's H-Bomb survival kit.

Another sign of the atomic age was ID bracelets that would identify the wearer in case of any emergency. The U.S. Bureau of Standards and the Federal Civil Defense Administration designed the identification bracelets which sold for 50 cents each. These bracelets were offered to all Long Beach school children and their families. Participation in the program was strictly voluntary. These ID tags included the name of the owner, his address, telephone number, blood type and religion. It also had a code number.

Clem Thy, who owned H & M Engraving in Long Beach, decided to include additional information related to the code in the 10x8-foot bomb shelter he was building in his back yard. The records, protected by a layer of concrete 10 to 16 inches thick, would be safe from all but a direct hit and would be available to civil defense workers. It would provide them with next of kin, employer or school, any illness from which the wearer suffered and an agreed upon meeting place for the wearer and family. The cost to erect Thy's shelter? $400 to $500.

In January 1960, Harry J. Krusz of the Long Beach Chamber of Commerce released a 55-page report advising the city what it needed to do to make the city a better place to live and work. Krusz criticized dirty downtown streets, shabby store fronts, resistance to progressive change, landlord public relations, planning conflicts, retired people who refused to remain young-in-heart, defeatism over land sinkage, antagonistic attitudes, empire building and special interest groups. But Krusz also found areas to praise including restaurants, schools, recreation, retail promotion, newspapers, potential leadership, and convention promotion. He concluded the city had "long-range potential."

Krusz, who wrote the analysis after interviewing 100 of Long Beach's civic leaders, felt there were too many small, organized groups in town who were just against things. He decried the blockage of a new City Master Plan by these groups stating the city needed a blueprint upon which to build.

Though the Krusz report specified that the citizens of Long Beach needed to be more progressive and not be against things, local folk were not going to change when it came to the issue of atomic waste.

In 1959, the Atomic Energy Commission designated several specific ocean sites for atomic dumping. Radioactive waste products were piling up quickly in vaults and needed to be disposed of before they became a problem in populated areas. A site 185 miles west-southwest of Long Beach was one of the areas chosen and for a while it looked like atomic waste products from all nuclear installations in the 11 Western states would be dumped into the Pacific Ocean off the Southland. The government assured everyone the process was safe: radioactive products would be packed in drums, and then weighed down with concrete several inches thick. The drums were designed to drop to 2,000 fathoms – an ocean bottom more than two miles below the surface of the Pacific. At first the AEC planned to use the Navy to do the dumping, instead they decided to license private companies to do the job. It was when Long Beach citizens found out that Coastwise Marine Disposal Company, at 2100 W. 15th Street, had gotten one of these contracts that trouble started.

Radioactive waste materials, too hot to handle as normal refuse, were being trucked to the heart of Long Beach's northwest industrial section from nuclear facilities throughout the west. When the warehouse became so loaded with drums of radioactive materials that the stockpile overflowed into the warehouse yard people began to get concerned. When counted, it was found that 6,000 containers were waiting dumping at sea.

Long Beach officials decided to rescind the company's business license, which it had gladly given in September 1959, and sent them back their $21 business license fee. The company was told to close up shop and get their A-waste out of town. Coastwise refused and Long Beach police blockaded the Coastwise yard, stopping a caravan of trucks bearing waste from Livermore. On January 13, 1960, the city used its police power to create 13 temporary radioactive waste storage "centers" – all truck trailers parked on a northwest Long Beach street for an indefinite stay. The trucks were loaded with 728 cement encased drums of waste from a Livermore laboratory. Now, instead of just one A-waste disposal center to watch there were 14. Coastwise could have unloaded the 13 trucks in a warehouse behind locked gates but the city refused the trucks entry, dispatching three police cruisers to guard the vehicles. Meanwhile, the AEC gave Coastwise a clean bill of health and praised Boswell for his safety program. It was costing Boswell $2600 a day until the trucks were unloaded and he would lose $250,000 in contracts if the City of Long Beach shut him down. Despite assurances by the AEC regarding safety, the city stuck to its decision.

On January 15, 1960, police authorized the trucks to unload 728 drums on a remote section of Pier A. A 24-hour guard was placed on them at Coastwise's expense. On January 26, 1960, the drums were allowed to be loaded by Coastwise for dumping at sea. Then court actions began.

Coastwise officials testified they had applied for an AEC license to dispose of A-waste in June 1959. No one from the city had protested since the AEC had high standards of safety with regard to the handling of nuclear waste. In September 1959 the city issued Coastwise a business license. Coastwise was inspected by the Fire Department in October. No complaint was filed, nor was there a complaint from the City Health Department. Suddenly, however, the operation became a "potential hazard" four months later. Why? Coastwise neighbors.

Area residents didn't buy owner Robert Boswell's claim that the containerized waste wasn't dangerous. If it wasn't dangerous why did they have danger signs on the barrels and dump it 185 miles out at sea? Besides, Eugene Field Elementary School was just down the street as were numerous meat packing businesses. What would the effect of even a small amount of radiation have on the food supply and students?

Others, such as Long Beach Junior Chamber of Commerce president Marvin H. Cheeks were appalled at the city's treatment of Coastwise claiming city councilmen obviously had stirred up radioactive hysteria to win votes, some even appearing on television which was calculated to create mass hysteria.

On March 19, 1960, the Superior court issued a restraining order against the City of Long Beach and ordered city hall to validate Coastwise's business license. The following day Coastwise received its first shipment of radioactive waste since January.

On March 26, 1960, a passerby on 15th Street heard a tremendous explosion and saw a 55-gallon metal drum shoot fifty feet into the air. Coastwise said an unknown chemical had been dumped into the empty drum and it reacted when water touched it. Owner Robert Boswell claimed it was sabotage, attributed to pranksters. Neighbors didn't think it was a prank when the drum ricocheted off the roof of the Coastwise plant then bounced onto the roof above a neighbor's bedroom before falling on a driveway. Boswell told the press his company used no chemicals, and all the drums were empty. The mystery was who dumped the chemical in the drum, and why?

Boswell later changed his mind as to who he thought was behind the explosion. It was no prank. He was sure Councilman Pat Ahern, his harshest critic, was behind the explosion. Boswell also criticized Long Beach newspapers for their unfair treatment of the company. The day before the blast the *Press-Telegram* reported Boswell had signed up to manage the campaign of city council candidate Ana Marie Peterson, who sought to out the incumbent in the 3rd District. Newspaper headlines told how Boswell hoped to dump the whole city council.

A few days later NBC television decided to see if the Atomic Energy Commission was right in stating a radium-dial watch gave off more radiation than one of Coastwise's atomic-waste drums. It did. Watch reading: .5 milliroetgens. Atomic-waste drums: .05. All was reported nationwide on the Huntley-Brinkley Report.

At a hearing held in May 1960, Boswell testified how the City of Long Beach forced Coastwise to violate some AEC rules. Boswell stated the majority of violations occurred in January when the city impounded 13 truckloads of atomic waste on Long Beach streets. The trucks were parked on open streets for three days under a police guard. AEC rules forbid holding up A-waste shipments. His testimony was for naught. In December 1960 his license was rejected by federal authorities.

On February 2, 1961, the Atomic Energy Commission issued orders closing Boswell's Coastwise Marine Disposal plant claiming drums containing waste were not properly labeled and the company was guilty of processing waste with higher radiation levels than regulations permitted. Coastwise was given 30 days to dispose of the waste, but the company declared bankruptcy. A San Pedro firm, California Salvage, its competition eliminated, petitioned the AEC to remove the drums. The Atomic Energy Commission agreed and California Salvage moved the 3,000 drums of radioactive waste from Coastwise's facilities and peeled off a layer of topsoil. The waste was trucked to Utah for underground disposal. Browning Automatic Forklift, took over the site at 2100 W. 15th Street in August 1961, after exhaustive tests by the AEC showed the site was free of radioactive waste.

In 1963, the United States and the Soviet Union signed the Limited Test Ban Treaty prohibiting nuclear testing in the air, space, or sea. One hundred twenty-six other countries also ratified the treaty. The initiative had been in the works for years but negotiations had repeatedly failed. Now that it was finally signed, testing moved underground. Neither superpower trusted the other to honor the commitment for very long; in fact, the number of tests per month actually increased after the treaty; the idea was to stay weapons-ready in the event one side broke the agreement.

On September 23, 1992, under the Nevada Test Site, the United States conducted its 1,030th, and last, nuclear weapon explosion. The Soviet Union had halted underground testing on October 24, 1990, the United Kingdom in 1991, China and France in 1996. Testing in North Korea still continues as of this writing, 2018.

Rock 'N' Roll

Long Beach has been a music mecca for over a century. Beginning in the 1880s it hosted Chautauqua events which included musical programs as well as instruction. In 1885 Long Beach added a branch of the Los Angeles Music conservatory to its list of educational institutions, and in 1909 it became the first town in America to fund a municipal band. It lured well known musical stars of the era to the city including Dame Melba, the Australian born operatic soprano with an international reputation, who Melba toast is named after. It was also home to opera star Marilyn Horne, a Poly High graduate. Another local lad, Spike Jones, put his own zany imprint on the music of a whole generation.

Jones was born Lindley Armstrong Jones in Long Beach on December 14, 1911. Attracted to music at an early age, he began his career at age ten when a friend whittled him a pair of drumsticks from wooden chair legs. At Poly High Jones was drum major of the school's 90-piece band and in his final high school years he headed his own combo called Spike Jones and His Five Tacks. Following graduation from Poly, Jones attended Chaffee Junior College. During this time he broke into the ranks of the big bands and started coming into contact with such names as Bing Crosby, Al Jolson, Eddie Cantor and Burns and Allen. One day he heard a pair of shoes squeak during the rendition of a number by a serious orchestra and the thought occurred to him that maybe he could inject a little comedy into music. Getting together a group of musician friends Jones threw out the trumpet notes and substituted gunshots. He discarded the piano for a couple of auto horns. Soon he was adding cowbells, kitchen utensils, dog barks and small cannon.

Jones was always coming up with something new. At one point, he brought in a toilet seat laced with strings and called it a "guitarlet." Another time he went so far as to have his trombone player burp at several pauses in a song. Besides dressing his band in outrageous costumes, he did whatever he could for a laugh. He once included a pretty girl harpist in his orchestra and had her do nothing but sit on a rocking chair and knit a scarf.

Jones embraced Calypso music and its use of bongo drums, which was an "in thing" for a while. In April 1957 music dealers around Long Beach reported brisk business in bongo drum sales among customers in the 14 to 40 age group. The craze caught most manufacturers of musical instruments off guard, and as such many drums had to be imported from Latin America to meet the demand. By the spring of 1957, however, there were three factories in the Long Beach area playing catch-up with the backlog of bongo orders.

The bongo ensemble consisted of two drums, one smaller than the other, which were bolted together. That was the basic outfit, usually ranging in price from $10.50 to $65. They appealed to the "beat generation" affectionately known as beatniks. Beatniks were stereotyped as wearing black turtleneck sweaters, berets, sandals, dark glass, and pounding on bongo drums as they read poetry.

Spike Jones' singular brand of music depended on something substantial and melodic. So when rock 'n' roll came in, he threw up his hands in despair. He is quoted as saying "how can you slaughter a tune that already is a mess."

Jones, who died on May 1, 1965, may have changed his mind if he had listened more closely to some of Long Beach's more recent home grown bands, some of which even adopted his antics.

Southern California had all kinds of subcultures, but the surfers stood out with their rugged mystiques and the sport's exotic history. The Pyramids, a local surf band formed in 1961, consisted of Skip Mercier (lead & rhythm guitar), Ron McMullen (drums), Tom Pitman (sax), Willie Glover (rhythm guitar) and Steve Leonard (bass), all students at Poly High who played rock 'n' roll on the side. The group happened to be at the right place at the right time. On September 1, 1961, *Life* magazine published a seven-page spread on surfing, which described it as "a way of life." A surfing obsession hit the nation with the Pyramids, the Beach Boys and many others cashing in on the trend.

The Pyramids' first break came in San Bernardino where they were playing for a dance sponsored by a local radio station. After their performance some of the dancers, along with the Deejays, suggested they record one infectious number that everyone wanted to hear repeated. That number was *Penetration.* The tune was the result of writer Steve Leonard's attempt to create an instrumental similar to The Chantays' *Pipeline.* He used the same basic compositional elements but placed them in a higher key, resulting in a similar but distinct tune. During the recording of *Penetration*, rhythm guitarist Willie Glover left the studio to eat while the others continued to work. The band's lead guitarist, Skip Mercier, recorded a rhythm guitar track and then half-serious, overdubbed his lead. By the time Glover returned to the studio, the tune was "in the can," and headed for a top Billboard chart position of #18 in February 1964. The song launched the boys on a nationwide tour.

Like the legendary Spike Jones, the teens entertained the audience with surprising shenanigans. For one number, a take-off on the Beatles, they wore wigs and trench coats that came off revealing nude heads and bright surfer trunks. Sometimes they'd arrive at their shows in a helicopter, and one time they pulled up in front of a ballroom on an elephant. In 1964, they appeared in the movie *Bikini Beach* wearing Beatles wigs. A fishing line from above jerked the mops straight off to reveal shaven baldy heads as the band began playing their song *Record Run.* The movie also had the group performing an instrumental, *Bikini Drag.* The Pyramids stopped performing in 1965.

Adrian and the Sunsets was another Long Beach band. Adrian Lloyd, born in Cornwall, England, moved to the United States and Long Beach when Lloyd was 15 years old. By the time he graduated from Poly High School in 1960 he was already playing in a local rock band, and in 1962 he joined the Rumblers. He left that group in 1963 and quickly put together a new band, Adrian and the Sunsets, which included guitarists Ron Eglit and Clyde Brown, bassist Dick Lambert and sax man Bruce Riddar. Adrian was the only one over 18. The group lasted for 11 months until they became disenchanted with their business manager and split up.

Adrian's fans gave him the unofficial title of the "Southland's Greatest Drummer," when he was playing for the Rumblers. Adrian also appeared on the same stage with Elvis Presley, Jan and Dean and the Olympics. *Breakthrough* was the name of Adrian's first album with his new group. It included selections such as *Wipe Out, Surfer Joe, Pipe Line* and *Boss.* It failed to chart, which was another reason the group disbanded. Later *Breakthrough* became one of the most sought-after collector's items among fans of classic era surf music. Lloyd went on to release a handful of solo singles and later joined the Playbacks.

Long Beach was also home to another "pop" group, who called themselves the Nitty Gritty Dirt Band. The band formed when Jeff Hanna and Bruce Kunkel met at Jordan High School. The two decided to head in a different direction than the surf music craze, and instead pursue their love of folk music. Like many other teenagers of then and today, they decided to form their own group which they called The New Coast Two. Later, as jug bands became popular, they changed their name to the Illegitimate Jug Band. They called it "illegitimate" because they did not use a jug.

In 1966, they formed the "Dirt Band" along with four other musicians they had met and "hung out" with at McCabe's Guitar Shop in Long Beach. Other "Dirt Band" members included Ralph Barr (guitar) and John McEuen (banjo) who both had attended Wilson High School, Jimmie Fadden (harmonica, jug, drums and washtub bass) a Millikan graduate, and Les Thompson (mandolin) who graduated from Garden Grove High School (but he was born in Long Beach). Jeff Hanna played washboard, sand blocks and comb and was the on-stage spokesman for the group. Bruce Kunkel, known as the "sex-symbol," played kazoo, guitar and washtub bass. Like Spike Jones before them, the group performed more than music. Donna Peters writing in the *Independent Press-Telegram* in 1967 had this to say about seeing them in action:

As the sextet ambles on stage and launches into a song with its traditional instruments and non-instruments, the audience is temporarily transported back to the 1920s. During one of the songs, Ralph takes out a bottle of pink solution and with it he blows bubbles. At the same time, John brings out a magic hat. A string of silver tinsel streams out of that hat for at least two minutes.

The group chose the unusual name when a political science professor at Long Beach City College stated during a lecture that "in order to get down to the real nitty gritty…" which seemed to strike the right chord in the group, and they decided to adopt "Nitty Gritty" as part of their name.

The young men, who bought their clothes at thrift stores, had a contract with Liberty Records. In 1967, following their first album, "The Nitty Gritty Dirt Band," they toured the country appearing on the Merv Griffin, Johnny Carson, Smothers Brothers and Joey Bishop shows. In May 1977 they were also the first American band to appear in the Soviet Union. They played 28 sold out concerts, and a televised appearance attracted 145 million people. The band has had many personnel changes, but original members Jeff Hanna, John McEuen and drummer Jimmie Fadden remain. The group celebrated their 50th anniversary in 2016 and continues to play along with newer member Bob Carpenter.

In 1967, Long Beach became home base for yet another aspiring pop music group – Aunt Dinah's Quilting Party. No, it wasn't a sewing circle playing pop music; it was a band of five men, all self-taught instrumentally, who played folk, folk-rock, jug band and bluegrass. The group included Ron LeGrand, a Long Beach native and Poly High grad, who started playing music in 1962 and was influenced by the Weavers and the Kingston Trio. He was the leader of the group and on-stage spokesman. Tom Mullen played all the string instruments as well as a washboard and lived in Pasadena. Tom Kuehl grew up in Phoenix, Arizona, and played guitar, harmonica and tambourine. Mel Durham, who lived in Long Beach, played bass, fiddle and guitar; his love was bluegrass. Richard McEuen, a Poly and USC grad, played guitar.

Ron, Tom Kuehl and Richard had played together for quite a while before Mel joined the group. They later added their mandolin player, Tom Mullen. The band used to be called the "Fly-By-Night Fleabag," but Disneyland, where they were performing, didn't like the name. So, faced with the decision of either changing their name or losing a job at the Magic Kingdom, they decided to change their name to a song they performed called *Aunt Dinah's Quilting Party.* They liked the sound of it and decided to keep it.

The group, who in 1967 appeared on the Andy Williams' Show, continued preforming folk songs and bluegrass through the 1970s, before disappearing from the music scene like so many other bands from their era.

One of the most popular Southland surf bands was *Dick Dale and the Del-Tones,* which attracted big crowds at the Rendezvous Ballroom in Balboa and at various venues throughout Long Beach.

Dick Dale had to struggle to convince folks at the Rendezvous to permit rock 'n' roll. It didn't help that the first night less than 40 kids showed up for the dance. It wasn't profitable and Dale was afraid he would lose his permit. He came up with the idea of approaching Newport Harbor High School and asked if the band could give a music demonstration to the students. A persuasive Dale got the school to agree to an early morning assembly with the stipulation that Dale play "nice" music. He agreed to their terms and even brought in a dancing couple for demonstrations. He held to his agreement until the last 15 minutes of the assembly when he mentioned that he and his band were playing at the Rendezvous later that evening. He then proceeded to play a short set of wild rock 'n' roll instrumentals, to the chagrin of the teachers, but to the delight of the students. Within three months of his appearance at the high school, Dick Dale and his Del-Tones were attracting over 4,000 kids per night to their dances.

Dale and the Del-Tones performed frequently in Long Beach. Dale was always generous. At the "Festival of Fun and Fashion" at the Long Beach arena in April 1963, the 22-year-old former metallurgist at Hughes Aircraft, presented records to the first 1,000 young persons who showed their student body cards. In July 1964, Dale and the Del-Tones, made two appearances in the Nu-Pike's Lido Ballroom, with all proceeds going to the American Cancer Society. Dale also donated a surfboard and hundreds of record albums to the cancer cause.

In an interview with Bob Thomas in April 1963, the guitarist who surfed every day said he wanted to improve the image of surfers. He was aware that some surfers had been labeled as troublemakers, and his goal was to improve the concept. Dale told Thomas:

The kids who attend my dances know that I won't stand for any fooling around. If I see someone smarting off, I stop the music and tell him to leave. They used to come to my dances barefoot and in tattered jeans. Now they dress respectably. They know how I feel; you can be a surfer and still look clean-cut. (Press-Telegram 4/10/1963)

However, Dale didn't sing. None of the surf songs had vocals, until Jan and Dean and the Beach Boys. However Dale noted for playing his percussive, heavy bending style, was so catapulting that listeners to his music would rise off the floor, chanting and stomping. It was the beginning of what came to be known as the surfer's stomp.

But music was also a vehicle used by Communists to indoctrinate the young, Long Beach's Fred Schwarz told the press in October 1964. "You'd be amazed at how much doctrine can be taught in one song." Pete Seeger was one example. When the clean-cut, Kingstone Trio released their rendition of Seeger's *Where Have All the Flowers Gone?* in 1962, about the senselessness of war and politicians blindness to its folly, many felt Marxist philosophy had succeeded in sinking its roots into American tradition. To combat this infiltration Schwarz introduced folk singing to his Christian Anti-Communism Crusade, by changing the lyrics to some songs such as *Blue Tail Fly:*

When I was young it seemed to me, the whole wide world would soon be free. But Communism is on the rise and Satan has a new disguise. Be careful of the Commie lies, swallow them and freedom dies. The U.S.A. must realize that she's the biggest prize. Why be surprised when they retreat, their major weapon is deceit. When will we learn, alas, alack, it's three steps forward, two steps back... (Los Angeles Times 10/14/1964)

Though many teens were aware of the Communist threat, they couldn't resist the singer the *Press-Telegram* described in 1956 as "America's Only Atomic-Powered Singer" – Elvis Presley.

Some historians mark Elvis Presley's arrival in the 1950s as a turning point in postwar American culture, not just because of his overt sexual energy expressed in his performances, but they claim his rebellious spirit anticipated the political unrest of the 1960s. Many disagree, pointing out that this new-fangled thing called rock 'n' roll didn't deal with politics, and that eventually Elvis would voice his support for Richard Nixon and Nixon's stance against Communism.

Also described as a "hillbilly rock and roller," 21-year-old Elvis Presley performed on stage at the Long Beach Municipal Auditorium on June 7, 1956. Sociologists denounced him as the outlet for mass teenage sex feelings. Clergymen called him a riot inciter. Parents described his act as obscene, indecent, savage, and degenerate. His fans, mostly teenaged girls, disagreed claiming grown-ups had forgotten how it feels to be young.

Despite the screams of 4000 teenagers, Elvis started his concert (tickets were $1.50 or $2.00) with *Heartbreak Hotel* – released in January 1956 and one of the biggest songs in the country at the time. The lyrics sung at the concert were virtually incomprehensible because of the screaming fans, but the rhythm got through, as did the bumps and grinds.

At times, usually when Elvis gyrated more than usual, the whole crowd screeched. Sometimes they surged towards the stage where a platoon of private police tried to keep the peace. Elvis went through half an hour of songs; favorites of the crowd included *Blue Suede Shoes* and *I've Got a Woman*.

Presley arrived at the auditorium in a new black Cadillac convertible, one of three which he owned. He wore a lavender checked sports coat, ruffled ivory shirt open at the neck and charcoal slacks that draped over his heals. He was accompanied by a statuesque blonde, with another blonde waiting backstage. After the show, the teenager idol flopped into a dressing room chair. When one young girl who had eluded guards managed to find him, the Mississippi boy smiled at her, but wouldn't let her in. Long Beach was lucky. In some cities, rock 'n' roll concerts and dances had touched off riots.

Rock 'n' roll was banned in Asbury Park, New Jersey, to prevent a reoccurrence of teenage riots that had occurred in June 1956. Radio station WMIN, in Saint Paul, Minnesota, announced in July 1956 it was permanently discontinuing all programming of rock 'n' roll and rhythm and blues records because of the recent outbreaks of violence in connection with this "type" of music. In San Antonio, Texas, rock 'n' roll was banned from swimming pool juke boxes because such music attracted an "undesirable element" of boys who didn't swim but danced with girls in swim suits.

Before the rock 'n' roll craze hit Long Beach, police on the amusement zone detail occasionally looked in on events in the auditorium from time to time. When the first rock 'n' roll dance was held 350 youths were turned away because a city ordinance forbid youngsters under 17 attending a public dance without their parents or guardians. By the fall of 1956 most teenagers knew they couldn't get in because of their age and didn't bother to try.

In September 1955, when local police sensed the threat of teenage violence at rock 'n' roll dances, special details were assigned to patrol them. When a promoter scheduled such an event at the

Municipal Auditorium, 16 regular police officers were assigned to keep the peace. These were made up of off-duty personnel and the dance promoter had to pay the cost of the officers' overtime. In addition, promotors also had to hire 10 private policemen to help keep enthusiasms in check.

Police said potential trouble surrounded those who tried to show off their own unique dance styles. To prevent any trouble Long Beach police stepped in and broke up the novel gyrations to the grumbling of the teenagers.

One psychologist at Long Beach State College said it was a group situation and a feeling of belonging to the group that pushed the success of rock 'n' roll. A clergyman said he could see no "evil significance" in rock 'n' roll, and saw it as a fad, comparable to some of the crazes of the 1920s. Would the fad continue? Opinion was divided. One record store manager said the craze was as strong as ever, another said the trend seemed to be going downhill and jazz appeared to be taking over.

One advantage for teenagers of the 1950s was that record stores had listening booths for them to hear the latest songs. Many came in and passed hours listening to the newest releases. Record store owners in 1956 didn't seem to mind too much, but in later years listening booths became a thing of the past.

On November 23, 1956, fifteen hundred girls, mostly teenagers, began lining up at 4:30 a.m. to get a seat for the 10 a.m. showing at the Fox West Coast Theater on Ocean Boulevard to see Elvis' first film – *Love Me Tender*. Some of the Long Beach girls were members of the Presleyettes of Southern California, who all wore pink pedal pushers and black sweaters lettered with the name of their club. Their official slogan was "to prove to the public that Elvis Presley is not a menace to the teenage morals." Each of the 85 Presleyettes had a snapshot taken with Elvis at the Beverly Wilshire Hotel where Presley stayed during his West Coast appearance earlier in the year. Though diligence, they found his phone number and called him every day. Finally he agreed to let the insistent fans take pictures of each other with him at the hotel.

As the girls lined up to get into the theater some leaned against a glass picture frame covering a billboard display and broke the glass. Before the film started, 15-year-old Beverly Rook president of the Presleyettes, asked the West Coast Theater manager if she could have a microphone to speak to the girls. Walking onto the stage she told the young audience they had not been good guests when they were out front waiting in line. She asked that they each chip in a nickel or a dime to pay for the broken glass picture frame. After the movie the theater manager handed the heavy bag of coins back to Beverly and asked that the club use the money to buy records or Presleyette sweaters.

The crowd screamed with glee when Presley appeared on screen singing his first number *We're Gonna Move*. Those in the front row slid down to the floor, rested on their knees and stared at the screen. When Elvis went into his second song, however, the audience maintained a deadly quiet as he sung his popular ballad, *Love Me Tender*. The theater management said the crowd had been noisy, but not in the least unruly.

Was rock 'n' roll here to stay? Elvis had competition such as Pat Boone, Tommy Sands and Tab Hunter. Where did Elvis rank? A nationwide survey conducted in March 1957 gave some interesting answers. The results were unanimous. Rock 'n' roll was as popular as ever and Elvis was still the most popular performer by a three-to-one majority, though his popularity rating had dropped from 35% to 21% since an October 1956 survey. Pat Boone was moving up in the ranks with nearly 13% of the youthful balloters. He was admired because he was supporting a family, going to school and pursing a singing career. Thirty-nine per cent of the boys and 33 per cent of the girls thought the Elvis craze would run its course within less than a year. Forty-two per cent of the girls and 31 per cent of the boys gave him from one to two years of peak popularity, 8.5 and 17 per cent respectively, figured two to four more years, while the rest thought

Elvis wouldn't fade for another four years. One girl said Elvis was popular, but a fad couldn't go on forever.

Surprising to some, the music also appealed to the older generation. One 49-year-old woman wrote and said Elvis was the best thing to hit the U.S. since Bing Crosby. But his most loyal fans were younger. One 14-year-old wrote that she had a mad crush on Elvis. She became so obsessed about him that her school work suffered and she didn't want anything to do with boys her own age. She said she was trying to get over her obsession; there were just too many other males who were available around.

Part of Elvis' and other rock 'n' rollers popularity sprang from their performances on the popular Ed Sullivan Show. The show, which started in 1948, was hosted by the top-flight Broadway and syndicated columnist who didn't sing, dance, act, smile or talk too well. But this lack of showbiz pizzazz was what made him so appealing, he was just like the average Joe. He did, however, have a knack for spotting good talent. Sullivan jump started the careers of Dean Martin and Jerry Lewis, Jackie Gleason, Sam Levenson, Marcel Marceau, Elvis Presley and the Beatles to name but a few. He was constantly on the lookout for new talent, traveling far and wide in search of new faces and acts. His show appealed to all ages, and, as such, an appearance on the Ed Sullivan show guaranteed success to almost any performer. However, Sullivan vowed to never allow Elvis on the show. When Elvis made appearances on the Steve Allen Show and Milton Berle Show and the ratings soared, Sullivan changed his mind. Elvis debuted on the Ed Sullivan Show on September 9, 1956, a second time on October 28, 1956, and the third and final appearance on January 6, 1957. For this final appearance Elvis was shown only from the waist on up.

In 1958 the king of rock 'n' roll was drafted, much to the distress of millions of fans. In his book *How we forget the Cold War*, John Wiener writes that Elvis mattered to both sides during the Cold War. The East Germans regarded him as a threat; the U.S. military saw him as an opportunity they could exploit. The East German

Communists feared him as "a means of seduction to make the youth ripe for atomic war."

To counter the Elvis "threat," the East Germans decided they needed to offer the youths of their country a substitute. They came up with the Lipsi, an alternative to Elvis' rock 'n' roll. Officially promoted as a couples dance, it was a kind of double-time waltz, where the man led and the woman followed. Politicians were worried that rock 'n' roll, where teens danced across from each other, promoted more gender equality and allowed more sexual expressiveness by women. However, the Lipsi didn't replace Elvis.

Elvis' stint in the military ended in 1960, and he went back to recording records and making films. But while he was just ending his time in the Army, one of rock music's most important performances took place at the Long Beach Municipal Auditorium on New Year's Eve in 1961. The event was a tribute for Richie Valens, the young Latino singer from the San Fernando Valley who in 1959 was killed in a plane crash that also claimed the lives of Buddy Holly and J.P. Richardson ("The Big Bopper). There were about ten acts, including Frankie Avalon, Della Reese, the Rivingtons, Ike Turner and the Ikettes. There was also a new group, whose song *Surfin'* (released in October 1961) had just entered radio station KFWB's Top 40 Survey at no. 33 – the Beach Boys.

The group, composed of Brian, Dennis and Carl Wilson, along with their cousin Mike Love and friend Al Jardine (David Marks later replaced Jardine), got their break from a contest sponsored by KDAY in the fall of 1961; the radio station played several songs, and whichever received the most call-in votes would be added to the playlist. *Surfin'* competed against *Duke of Earl*, and others, and with all the Wilson and Love family calling in multiple times, pushed *Surfin'* to victory.

Having made it to radio, the group, which originally wanted their names to be the "Pendletones", was now a real band, and that meant playing in front of live audiences. The boys were really youngsters, Mike Love the oldest at twenty, Carl the youngest at fourteen. The

New Year's Eve program in Long Beach was their third performance and they were petrified, according to Mike Love, of having to appear after Ike Turner and the Ikettes who were sexy and charismatic and in complete command of the audience. Somehow the boys made it through *Surfin'*, *Johnny B. Goode*, and one other song. They also were amazed that they were paid $60 each. Mike Love recalled it was amazing to him that he had to work eight hours a day at a sheet metal factory to make anything close to $60 and now he got paid for singing three songs.

Despite intense competition from other surf bands, the Beach Boys (without all the original members) are still performing today. By the dint of their lyrics, distinctive harmonies, and timings they have come to embody the "California" sound.

What of Elvis? Inadvertently he played a major role in the popularity of the beach film genre. In his 1961 film *Blue Hawaii*, Elvis portrayed a beach boy surf instructor. It turned out to be the biggest box offices smash of any Presley movie. In turn, Elvis would rehash his *Blue Hawaii* role, returning to the surf theme in *Girls! Girls! Girls!* (1962) and *Paradise, Hawaiian Style* (1966).

The king of rock 'n' roll paid a return visit to Long Beach on Valentine's Day 1964 to present a caring gift to St. Jude's Hospital in Memphis. But you may be wondering what was Elvis (who was from Memphis) doing in Long Beach to present a gift to a Memphis hospital? It was the gift – Franklin Delano Roosevelt's presidential yacht *Potomac*, which Elvis had purchased in January at public auction for $55,000. Presley first offered it to the March of Dimes as a gift, but the organization said it had no funds for the vessel's upkeep and turned the gift down. Presley then offered it to the U.S. Coast Guard Auxiliary, ostensibly because the bill bringing the auxiliary into existence was signed aboard the vessel. The Coast Guard also turned it down. Now Presley had found someone willing to accept his gift – St. Jude's Hospital.

Elvis' retinue of publicity men and 20 uniformed officers were swarming over Berth 73 in Long Beach harbor putting up bunting and signs and special walkways, in preparation for his 1 p.m. donation to St. Jude's Hospital in Memphis. The ceremony was almost called off when the property owner, Llewellyn Bixby, showed up and informed the group he hadn't given permission for use of the dock. Bixby said he was worried about public liability. Colonel Tom Parker, Presley's manager, said he thought an earlier lease with an auction company covered the ceremonies. After a conference with Bixby, Parker promised to pay for a special $500,000 liability insurance policy and to keep the public off the dock. Actor Danny Thomas was there to accept the gift on behalf of the hospital. Thomas said it was hoped someone would buy the ship and preserve it as a historic shrine. It was. It is now preserved by the Potomac Association in Oakland, California, open to dockside visits and regular cruises on San Francisco Bay.

Though several teen-age girls appeared early in front of the dock on West Seventh Street, waiting for Elvis' arrival, it appeared as if the King of Rock 'n' Roll had competition, not only from the Beach Boys but from the Beatles.

Americans weren't the only ones making musical history. There was another group about to define rock 'n' roll, and it came from across the Atlantic – the Beatles.

In February 1964 Beatle mania hit Long Beach and the rest of the U.S. The "Fab Four" – John, Paul, George and Ringo – had left London on February 7, 1964, with an estimated 4000 fans there to see them off. Another 3000 American fans greeted them in New York, pelting them with jelly beans and candy kisses. Fifteen months earlier they were playing in a Liverpool jazz cellar for about $20 a week. They now commanded $10,000 a performance and were reported to have already earned $17 million. They were here to appear on the Ed Sullivan show on February 9th, followed by a concert tour ending February 17th in Miami Beach.

I was a devoted Beatles fan, and sorry that I didn't live on the east coast to try to get a ticket to one of their shows. I wasn't the only one who loved them – only 721 out of 50,000 fans requesting tickets, were able to attend the Ed Sullivan Show. I had "discovered" them the previous year and played their song *I Want to Hold Your Hand*, over and over until the record wore out! Unfortunately, I was not able to attend their first (and only) Los Angeles concert on August 23, 1964, at the Hollywood Bowl. Instead I had to settle for joining hundreds of fans who stood in line for hours on the opening day of their first movie – *A Hard Day's Night*. There was lots of screaming, and crying as our favorite Beatle appeared on screen (my favorite was George). Among my group of friends we all had to choose a different Beatle as our favorite so we wouldn't fight over them.

If you had asked anyone in Long Beach about the Beatles a year earlier, they would have told you a beetle was a bug, not a rock group. Now everyone was going out buying a Beatle wig, in fact the Long Beach Broadway Department Store's first supply of wigs sold out in one day. There were also Beatle sweatshirts, Beatle T-shirts, Beatle autographs, and Beatle jewelry, scarves, hats and dolls. The *Wall Street Journal* reported that U.S. teen-agers would spend $50 million in 1964 alone on Beatle novelties. And the haircuts? Long Beach barbers didn't believe the fad would continue. Predictions were that by the time men here had grown enough hair the Beatles would have become has-beens. But one Long Beach band, the Pyramids, decided to defy Beatlemania by shaving their heads.

Though the Beatles never appeared in Long Beach, the Rolling Stones did. On May 16, 1965, the Stones were in town for a concert, and the crowd was kept under control during the musical portion of the show. It was afterwards that things got ugly.

Four thousand fans who had listened to the British group sing and stomp inside the Arena burst out the back exit and inundated a small, black station wagon which had been "hidden" for a speedy getaway. In the crush, 10 boys and girls were scratched, shoved, bruised and beaten; three police officers were clawed, kicked and practically stripped, and the getaway car was damaged. But the Rolling Stones escaped uninjured.

The plan had been for the Stones to be whisked through the Arena's back area to the waiting car where security officers and policemen would calmly handle their departure. But along the line a security leak developed, and when the last note was sung on stage not only the Stones whizzed through the Arena's back exits, but scores of pushing and pounding fans.

The car was surrounded, motorcycles were knocked to the ground, unsuspecting spectators found themselves shoved into the Stones, the policemen, the car and onto the ground. Then things started to fly through the air: cosmetics, shoes, purses, wallets, lipsticks, bottles and even some underclothing. Officers John Turley and Jim Reed jumped on top of the Stones' vehicle and began clearing the yelling fans from in front of the path of the vehicle to get the way cleared. Turley suffered ripped clothes and bruises to his legs as he hung onto the top of the car which now had its front lights broken out and luggage rack torn off, when it sped away from the Arena with a motorcycle escort. Another officer, D.L. Goldsmith, suffered a cut hand and lost his shirt to the mob. Seven unidentified girls were taken to St. Mary's Hospital in ambulances after they sustained minor injuries in the crush of the mob. A 17-year-old boy required two stitches to his head. But the Stones got away unharmed, boarding a helicopter as a running crowd of girls ran across the beach in an attempt to reach the craft.

Growing up in Long Beach in the 1960s, the most popular place to go for live entertainment was the Cinnamon Cinder. Opening on December 6, 1962, it replaced the La Ronda Rue Supper Club at the Traffic Circle which had once been the hang out of the teens' parents.

On opening night 500 youngsters danced deliriously inside while 350 disappointed others lined up outside, unable to get in because the place was jammed. The Beach Boys were the opening act. The Twist was the rage at the time and hundreds of young people twisted all night long. But fads come and they go, the Twist was replaced by the

Stomp, followed by the Bounce, the Shuffle, and Mashed Potato. On weekends the Cinder drew 600 to 800 dancers, most 18 to 20. Only 25 percent came as couples, the rest went "stag," arriving in groups of two, three or four.

Occasionally guest stars would visit such as the Righteous Brothers, the Pyramids, Dick and Dee Dee, Dick Dale and the Del-Tones, Jan and Dean, the Beach Boys, and more. The Cinnamon Cinder was the brain child of disc jockey Bob Eubanks and his partners who opened the original Cinder in Studio City in 1962. This was followed by other Cinders around the country.

The secret of the Cinder's success was an adherence to strict regulations – no youngsters under 18 were permitted. Single men past of the age of 25 were strongly discouraged and girls were not permitted if they were wearing capris or shorts. Boys were barred if they were wearing T-shirts, sweat pants, shorts, club or school jackets, Levis or tennis shoes. No alcoholic beverages were served. Persons with alcohol on their breath were stopped at the door. Admission was $1.50 and if a person left he or she had to pay an additional $1.50 to get back in. This was to discourage youngsters from going out to their cars and taking a sip of liquor! If someone tried to break the regulation they were permanently barred from the premises.

Some tried to sneak in. The most tempting route at the Long Beach Cinder was over a six foot fence which ran for approximately 100 feet along the Cinder's north side. As soon as a person climbed over it, however, he ran into an infra-red beam, invisible in the dark, which would shine along the top of the entire fence. As soon as the would-be intruder broke the beam, signal lights at a security station would light up and guards would rush to nab the culprit.

Within a year of opening the Long Beach Cinder had attracted over 150,000 paid admissions. The manager was Mickey Brown, a former police officer, who knew what kids liked – loud music. Brown had no problems with high decibel performances, he allowed bands to play as loudly as they would like.

The Cinder was a place for young people to meet, and in some cases this meeting led to marriage, such as the case of Jancane Diane

Smith and Gary Carl Boulton who met at the Cinder in 1963 and were married in 1967.

The Cinnamon Cinder wasn't the only place for the young to hang out. By 1964 the Lido Ballroom, which had been on the Pike since 1906, converted to the new wave sounds. Every Friday, Saturday and Sunday nights they featured music by a Long Beach surf instrumental combo the Illusions, which had a hit song in *Jezabel* and later *Night Mare*. At the Lido girls were admitted free on Friday and Saturdays from 8:30 until 9:00, and on Sundays from 7:30 until 8:00. After these times the admission price was $1. The Lido stressed "proper supervision" and "parents welcome." No jeans, capris, T-shirts or liquor were allowed on the premises.

Drummer Tom Brown and guitarist Larry Ellis formed the Illusions during the summer of 1962. The group also featured Gary Dodson (rhythm guitar), Colin Clark (piano), Bob Mason (guitar) and Roy Alvila (sax). While working at a small teen club in Bellflower called The Peppermint Lounge, they occasionally saw Dick Dale perform. Dale inspired the group to practice harder, develop the surfing sound, and work on original material. The band's lead guitarist, Bob Mason, took Dale's advice. He came across a 1951 record by Frankie Lane, called *Jezabel*. He reworked it into a stunning surf instrumental.

While performing in Long Beach, the Illusions were heard by local radio deejay George Huggins. Huggins took the band into a recording studio early in 1963 and they recorded *Jezabel*. According to Brown, it was done live, without overdubs, using one microphone! It was also recorded without a bass player, since the band simply didn't feel they needed one.

Other teen hang-outs included the Gay 90's (2508 Palm Drive in Signal Hill), the Marina Palace in Seal Beach, and the Soul Club (3118 E. South Street in Lakewood). The Soul Club, which opened April 6, 1967, described itself as an under 21, non-liquor rhythm and dancing center, designed exclusively for young folk aged 17 through 20.

The Soul Club didn't have an auspicious opening. The rain was heavy and nearly 200 youngsters turned up early in the evening with more expected. The attraction was the Saxtons, Millikan High's rock 'n' roll band which won second place while competing in the Pepsi-Cola Boss Battle of the Bands over a Los Angeles television station. As if standing in line in drenching rain wasn't enough, bad news followed. Almost at the last minute, the club owners learned that a Lakewood ordinance prohibited youngsters under 18 from dancing in a place where people over 18 were dancing. Reluctantly, the club's entertainment director stationed himself at the door and informed the 17-year-olds they couldn't come in.

It was a pitiful scene, reporter Tedd Thomey wrote, as scores of young girls and their escorts milled around in the rain, raising their voices in loud protest. They couldn't believe they weren't welcome. Waving damp one dollar bills in their hands (the price of admission) they demanding to be let in. During the evening the Soul Club turned away 150 disappointed teens. Confusion was rampant because the young people were well aware that other young adult centers, such as the Cinnamon Cinder in Long Beach, admitted 17-year-olds.

The following week the club owners obtained a waiver from the Lakewood city council which permitted the club to admit youngsters aged 15 through 20. The club reopened on April 14, 1967, again featuring the beat of the Saxtons, with vocal numbers by Johnny Angel. Johnny, born in Long Beach attended Jordan and Poly high schools and began his singing career when he was 15. He had performed with many of the Southland's leading groups such as the Coasters, Drifters, Little Richard and Ike and Tina Turner.

Eight years after it opened the Cinnamon Cinder was as empty as the dying La Ronde Rue it had replaced. The Soul Club was already gone. In a final effort to save the Cinder, Mickey Brown turned the building into a new nightclub called the Insider in December 1970. He obtained a liquor license, in hopes of luring an older crowd. He planned to pump more money into the business but the Bixby Land

Company decided to lease the property to Toyota at a higher rent. In came the wrecking ball and the club was gone.

The Cinnamon Cinder had been part of a West Coast chain of young adult nightclubs that stretched as far as Alaska. It went into decline, with the rise of rock concerts and a change of youth styles. *Press-Telegram* reporter Charles Sutton wrote: "the long-haired kids who attend rock concerts these days – long hair was frowned on at the Cinder, incidentally – are far less interested in dancing to music than they are in listening to it and smoking pot." Besides that, there were economic factors, performers were requesting higher fees, and the cost of admission went up.

All that remains of the Cinder are memories. The lot on which the club stood at 4401 E. Pacific Coast Highway was part of the old Bixby ranch. During World War II the Bixbys sold it to an Ormond St. Claire, who built a drive-in restaurant on the site. After the war the St. Claires added a wing and turned it into a nightclub. The land was later sold back to the Bixbys, who in turn leased it to Forest Smith, who turned it into the La Ronde Rue which eventually became the Cinnamon Cinder. The land remained a Toyota agency until 2017; a Chick-fil-A restaurant and other small businesses have gone into what is now a strip mall.

The longest lasting teen club in our area was the Marina Palace in Seal Beach. It opened in 1964, replacing the Airport Club which had been on a lot next to the San Gabriel River on the Orange County/Los Angeles County border since 1949. The club hosted teen dancing for 14 through 18 year olds from 8 p.m. to midnight. Many well-known groups appeared there. Despite allegations of immoral conduct, alcohol, drugs and lack of supervision, it stayed open until 1974 when the lease ran out. The Quonset buildings were torn down in the fall of 1975 and the site remains empty to this day.

Though the teen clubs are gone the memories remain of a time when music provided the soundtrack to this special time in American history.

A Murderous Instrument

For millions of young children during the 1950s and 60s learning to play the accordion was all the rage. Besides the surf and rock 'n' roll bands discussed earlier, there was Lawrence Welk and his orchestra, which was featured on television from 1951 to 1982 (and on present day PBS reruns of the show). Welk, who played the accordion, had been delighting audiences since the 1930s. In 1950 he added another accordion virtuoso, Myron Floren, to the band. The orchestra was a frequent attraction at the Long Beach Municipal Auditorium and in 1950s locals got to meet Welk and his featured soloists as they signed autographs at the Sears store at 5ᵗʰ and Long Beach Boulevard. Welk was the originator of that bouncing, effervescent "Champagne Music," a name that stuck as the group became known as Lawrence Welk and his Champagne Music Orchestra. His ensemble was so popular that it won the *Independent Press-Telegram's* TV popularity poll (which ran from 1951-1956) four years in a row from 1952-1956.

One Long Beach youth who took up the accordion, as well as dancing and singing, was Bobby Burgess whose talents led him to donning the ears of a Mouseketeer on the Mickey Mouse Club, and later to become a performer on the Lawrence Welk show. Burgess began dancing lessons at age three, and at age ten became a *Press-Telegram* newspaper boy. He joined the Disney Mouseketeers at age fourteen, and attended a studio school until his senior year when he returned to Long Beach Poly High School, graduating in 1959. While attending Long Beach State University he and Barbara Boylan (also from Long Beach) entered a dance contest held by Lawrence Welk.

Bobby and Barbara had met while they both took dance lessons at Call's Fine Art Center, a popular Long Beach dancing school. In 1961 they won Welk's contest which led to an appearance on The Lawrence Welk Show. They were such a tremendous success Welk hired the duo as permanent members of the show. Boylan, the first of Bobby Burgess' three dancing partners, left the act in 1967 when she married. Burgess remained with the show until 1982 when the program went off the air. In 1971 he married Kristin Floren, the daughter of Welk accordionist Myron Floren.

The accordion was the perfect keyboard instrument for the small sized, mass produced housing sweeping the country – the accordion took up little room and was less expensive than a piano. In Long Beach, accordion festivals were held at the Municipal Auditorium as accordionists from all over the nation came and competed (the author included).

Inspired by Lawrence Welk and others, learning to play the accordion became the cool thing to do. In 1938 the American Accordionists' Association (AAA) was founded. The group's goal was to show the public that the instrument was as serious as any other; by the 1950s the group had succeeded – the accordion was one of the most studied instruments in the country.

The Humphreys' Building at 132 Pine Avenue in Long Beach was a popular place to learn to play a musical instrument. The building housed 10 music teachers, including accordion instructor Violet Berling in unit 313. But for one youngster, the instrument she loved led to her death.

On October 12, 1950, a ten-year-old Long Beach girl died after being found bound with leather thongs in a chair in the apartment of an accordion teacher with whom she lived. Her body, found at 132 Pine Avenue, was covered with cuts, burns and bruises, some new and some old. The music teacher, Violet John Berling, told officers that little Katherine (Kay) Frances Erickson often inflicted injuries on herself with sharp instruments. She said the girl had abnormal interests in the occult and believed she had the power to heal. Berling swore Kay Frances had bound herself to the chair in which Berling found her that October morning. It was up to the defense to prove Berling right. They hoped to show that Kay Frances was addicted to trances, self-mutilation and abnormal practices and had inflicted wounds upon herself.

The child's mother admitted that on occasion the girl had deliberately caused herself bodily harm, but that Kay Frances just did it to get attention. Beatrice Erickson didn't feel there was anything occult about it. Mrs. Erickson did admit she took Kay Frances to spiritualist services, but that her daughter wasn't overly interested in the occult. During these services spirit trumpets and divining rods were used in the service. Berling later testified that these beliefs had a negative effect on Kay Frances.

After a man whom Berling said sexually abused Kay Frances died, the young girl started to put a rolled newspaper to her ear, imitating the spirit trumpets she had seen at séances, to listen to voices. Violet Berling said the child lived with her because a psychiatrist hoped music and a change of environment would help the young girl overcome her mental instability. She said that Kay Frances sometimes stared into space and would not answer when spoken to. Berling did take Kay Frances to a medical doctor for treatment of an infected finger several times. Dr. Wayne Hanson testified the child would not keep a bandage on the finger and when he asked her why she told him to "shut up." Before that when he questioned her she had remained silent.

Beatrice Erickson explained that the reason Kay Frances was living with Berling was that Harry Erickson had just gotten a job at the Navy shipyard in San Diego, and she needed someone to look after the child while she trained as a nurse. Kay Frances had been taking accordion lessons with Berling since June 1948, and the Ericksons trusted Berling to look after their daughter. For much of their marriage Harry Erickson was unemployed, and his wife worked to support the family. Now, with her husband working, Beatrice decided to become a nurse. During her training she was on call at all hours and with her husband away she needed someone to care for her daughter.

Mrs. Erickson said Kay Frances didn't like school, in fact the child had failed 4th grade; all she liked to do was play the accordion, and she wanted to become an accordion star. When she told her parents she wished to stay with Miss Berling all the time, the Ericksons talked it over and agreed.

Why would parents seemingly abandon their child to another and why had the mother only seen her daughter once in the three months preceding Kay Frances' death? Berling said Mrs. Erickson would only come to see the child when the spiritual "current" was right. At her trial, the fact that Violet Berling agreed to be Kay Frances' private tutor so the child wouldn't have to go to school, that she hadn't been paid for lessons since 1949, and the fact that she didn't receive any money from the parents for taking care of the child was brought into question.

Kay Frances wasn't the only student Violet Berling taught. In preparation for accordion competitions, Violet Berling formed a children's accordion quartette consisting of Kay Frances and three other children, who came to the studio to practice several times a week after school. Often one or more of the children stayed all night. One claimed they sometimes saw Kay Frances dripping with blood.

At Berling's trial, a 9-year-old student of Berling's said she and other pupils were fearful that "dreadful things" would happen to them if they told of the beatings Violet Berling administered to Kay Frances. The blond headed child told the court that blood dripping from cuts on Kay Frances' legs stained Kay Frances' clothing and formed pools on the floor of the music studio. The young girl said she never asked Kay Frances how she got the wounds, but Kay Frances was brave; she never cried or said her injuries hurt. The student did say Kay Frances showed her how she healed herself of wounds by rubbing her hands over them.

Upon cross examination by Berling's attorney, Albert Ramsey, the child witness reversed her account of Kay Frances' injuries and Berling's abuse. The young girl admitted she and her mother hated

Violet Berling. They had already concluded Violet had caused Kay Frances' death. It was decided by the prosecution not to call the other two students to the stand.

It was around 6:30 a.m. on October 12, 1950, in answer to a telephone call, that the fire department ambulance went to Berling's studio and found the body of Kay Frances Erickson lying on a studio couch. Violet Berling told police she woke up around six a.m. and found the child seated on a chair in the corner of the studio. Her hands and ankles were bound with leather straps and the girl mumbled for Miss Berling to take the accordion from her lap. Berling believed the girl had applied the straps herself. Seeing the child's condition, Berling called an ambulance which rushed Kay Frances to the hospital where she was pronounced dead. Death, the autopsy found, resulted from strangling on food and vomiting.

Berling claimed Kay Frances was alive when wheeled out of the studio on a stretcher, and that the aspiration of food may have occurred when the ambulance attendants attempted artificial respiration. However, an autopsy revealed Kay Frances had some injuries which could not have been self-inflicted and that the time of death was around 1 a.m. She could not have been alive at 6 a.m. when Berling claimed she heard the young girl speak.

The coroner ruled that none of the wounds were self-inflicted. Some were recent, others were reopened older wounds. Some were caused by a sharp instrument such as a razor blade; some had been inflicted only a short time before the 10-year-old's death. A number of burns had also been recently made. A stretching in Kay Frances' pubic area led the coroner saying this indicated a frequent stretching of the parts over some period of time, and the introduction of some object "of considerable resistance." As a result of these findings, Violet John Berling was arrested for the torture-murder of little Kay Frances Erickson. When Berling was taken to jail it was observed she had three long scratches extending from her left shoulder inward toward her chest and various other bruises over her body. Berling explained the scratches came from her accordion strap, something many found hard to believe.

The bizarre nature of the case attracted media attention from around the world. It would become one of the longest trials in the history of Los Angeles County. During Berling's hearing, Miguel Verdugo the music studio owner, agreed to testify only if he was granted freedom from prosecution. The press quickly picked up on their relationship, describing the more than 100 love letters he wrote to Violet which were confiscated from her apartment. Most were written to Berling in 1946 while Verdugo was in Las Vegas obtaining a divorce. Why didn't they marry? Verdugo told the press he just "cooled off." It was later determined Verdugo's letters had no relationship to the trial. But more interesting tidbits were added to the story when 54-year-old Miguel Verdugo proposed marriage to the 32-year-old Bering while she was in jail.

Verdugo told the court he had seen the child abuse herself sexually and bump her head against the wall. He said he saw Kay Frances Erickson strapped to chairs and frequently taped with heavy gauze bandages around her mouth and head. Verdugo told of sometimes taking Violet and several of her students out to dinner. Kay Frances did not always accompany the group, and when she was left in the studio she was tied to a chair by Berling.

Violet Berling refuted Verdugo's claims telling the court it was Verdugo who wouldn't allow Kay Frances to go with them for meals because of her bruises, and Verdugo who insisted Kay Frances be tied to a chair or filing cabinet when they went to dinner. Berling told the court that Verdugo once whipped Berling with his belt when Berling tried to stop him from punishing Kay Frances.

Violet Berling testified Beatrice Erickson had asked her to keep the young girl because the mother was afraid to leave Kay Frances at home with the child's father who had molested the young girl on previous occasions. Berling agreed to let her accordion pupil move in with her to help the mother out. Berling went on to tell the court that Kay Frances hated her parents and wanted to kill them by turning on the gas. When studio owner Miguel Verdugo heard Kay Frances say this he gave Kay Frances a whipping with a leather strap. Later Beatrice Erickson denied her husband ever molested Kay Frances or that she had given permission for her daughter to be physically punished.

Berling described how Kay Frances beat her head against the wall and on a chair, bit her hand, burned herself with a flatiron and rubbed her body on furniture. The child also walked in her sleep and apparently went into trances. When Violet told Beatrice Erickson about all this the mother said Mrs. Henry Decker (a family friend) probably was practicing black magic on Kay Frances. Berling asked Beatrice about taking the girl to a doctor for her injuries, but the mother refused. Only later when the wounds became infected did Berling ignore the mother's wishes and seek medical attention. Berling went on to add that the only time she saw Kay Frances cry was when she threatened to take her back to her parents.

The accordion instructor said it was standard practice to tie both adult and young students to a chair when they were playing heavy accordions. This allowed pupils better balance and freer use of their hands. Berling said Kay Frances often tied herself in the chair for the same purpose. She testified the young girl began fastening accordion straps around her wrists and ankles in an attempt to do acrobatic stunts after she became interested in a trapeze act she saw in a vaudeville show.

On March 16, 1951, Berling showed the jury how she tied Kay Frances and other pupils to a chair to aid them in balancing a heavy accordion. She fastened Kay Frances' orange-colored, 12-bass piano-accordion on her attorney, Albert Ramsey, with the accordion straps buckled in the back. Ramsey demonstrated what was done. He seated himself in the chair in which prosecutors said the child died. Berling took one of her scarfs entered in evidence, passed it around Ramsey's body underneath the accordion, over his left arm and tied it behind the back panel of the chair with a tight knot. Berling asked Ramsey if he could feel the weight of the accordion and he replied in the negative. Berling said it was because the weight of the accordion was on his chest, if it wasn't tied the weight would be heavy on his legs.

The left arm, Berling said, needed to be tied so the elbow would not fly up and out in working the accordion bellows.

During sixteen days on the witness stand, Violet Berling revealed that following the death of a family friend Kay Frances began going into trances. Sometimes she had other children take hold of Kay Frances' hands and run around with her to arouse her from her stupor. Often this was not enough, and a shake or slap across the face was necessary to bring her around. Violet said Kay Frances also used to walk in her sleep, as if in a trance, and once put on an accordion and tried to practice.

The testimony was so traumatic for Violet that she collapsed eleven times before ending her tale, but the State didn't grant her any sympathy. They asked the jury for a verdict of first degree murder under the January 5, 1950, amendment to the Penal Code. This amendment made death by lewd and lascivious conduct upon a child under 14 years of age murder in the first degree. Under their interpretation of the law it was murder in the first degree whether these acts were committed for the satisfaction of the person committing them or the person receiving them. Though Kay Frances had died from choking on regurgitated food, the doctor who performed the autopsy said that if she hadn't choked she would have soon died from other injuries. The prosecution charged that Violet Berling had inflicted the injuries in a sadistic homosexual frenzy.

Berling's attorney tried to convince the jury that all of the evidence was circumstantial. Was Berling a homosexual because she wore her hair in an odd bun on top of her head, which the prosecution said was masculine? What about the fact there was not one pair of slacks in her apartment, or that she wore silk stockings? What of her relationship with Verdugo? Ramsey also pointed out the autopsy done by coroner Dr. Victor Cefalu had used three methods of determining the time of death. Dr. Cefalu had stated that each of the three methods was inaccurate, but he insisted that together they gave an accurate answer. How could this be? How could Dr. Cefalu know that Kay Frances had vomited because of multiple injuries when everyone knew children could vomit for any reason? He also pointed out Kay Frances could have died in the ambulance. There was a damp spot on the ambulance sheet under the middle of the young girl's back. There was no open wound anywhere near it. It was perspiration. She was on a respirator for 15 minutes; she could have died during this time.

Ramsey also told how prosecuting attorney Ted Sten and the police had questioned Violet Berling for more than 3 hours following Kay Frances' death. During that time they never allowed Berling to call an attorney. Ramsey stated that Sten had threatened and harassed his client into saying just what Sten wanted to hear. In his final arguments Ramsey said:

There seems to me to be a great effort to free everyone of guilt in this case but this defendant. This is a murder trial by imagination... The birth certificate given Mrs. Erickson when Kay Frances was born showed she had another child who was alive...what did she do, give that child away as she did Kay Frances? Why did Miss Berling help Kay Frances? Do you have to have a reason to help little kids? (Press-Telegram 4/20/1951)

In reading the testimony myself I found one thing Ramsey failed to put together in Berling's defense – that Violet Berling identified with Kay Frances and wanted to help. Could it have been that Berling was just trying to aid another victim who had a mother who "acted strangely?"

Interestingly, Berling's mother, Mary Schauer, was called to the stand not by the defense but by the prosecution. When asked about the different surname, Schauer explained that she was separated from her husband and used her mother's maiden name instead of Berling. It was the name she used when she performed in Vienna as a singer and dancer before coming to the United States in 1911. The prosecution made much of the fact that she called her daughter "my little boy" and referred to her as "Johnnie." Sten and his team also pointed out that Berling had tried for several years to avoid her mother. They sought to prove that Berling was embarrassed because her mother was just a house maid. Berling did admit to trying to get away from her mother who, she stated, "acted strangely." In the end, Schauer proved to be an unreliable witness. After a few questions she became hysterical and was unable to proceed. Two years later Mary Schauer was admitted to a mental hospital.

Perhaps Violet Berling saw much of her mother in Beatrice Erickson, Kay Frances' mom. Besides changing their testimony in court, both were very religious, given to hysterics, and Mrs. Erickson also "acted strangely," according to Berling. Berling testified that Beatrice told her that Kay Frances was born dead and her friend Mrs. Decker had brought her back to life and Decker was now teaching Kay Frances to heal. Beatrice Erickson also told Berling that Mrs. Decker could tell her things even in the middle of the night when they were miles apart. When a doctor suggested the child be taken to a psychiatrist, Mrs. Erickson refused because the whole family would be involved. She claimed her husband acted "peculiar" around the house and she didn't want the psychiatrist to find out about him.

Prosecuting attorney Ted C. Sten found it impossible to believe that Violet Berling would take on total care of a child without compensation from the parents. The reason, Sten told the jury, was that Violet was a homosexual sadist. Her payment was in seeing Kay Frances suffer. He described Berling's story as the "greatest hoax and fraud" and charged that Ramsey "double-talked and misstated evidence during the trial." Sten ended by drawing a tombstone on the blackboard and wrote on it: "Kay Frances Erickson, 1940-1950. Murdered by a friend."

After eight days of deliberation, a grim-faced jury of seven men and five women concurred with the prosecution. Violet John Berling was found guilty of first-degree murder and sentenced to life imprisonment. Violet appeared amazed at their decision. "How could they do this to me? I never hurt any child," she asked in bewilderment. The trial, which began January 3, 1951, lasted 17 weeks – the longest murder trial in Los Angeles County's history up to that time. It cost taxpayers $46,800.

Two years later, Berling's lawyers used a bizarre argument to win her a retrial. Because she had fainted so often during the trial, she was "mentally absent," they said. In his decision, the judge wrote: "the conviction cannot be approved because of the violation of the defendant's fundamental right to be present physically and mentally and fully conscious during all stages of the trial." On May 8, 1953, after a swift one-day court trial, Judge George Francis found Violet guilty of second-degree murder. He was satisfied that Berling had inflicted torture on the girl, but said it couldn't be proven "beyond a reasonable doubt" that the wounds cause the child's death. The prosecution described Kay Frances' death as "a medieval sacrificial ceremony in which this woman used a child to gratify her abnormal sex drive." The 34-year-old music teacher was immediately sentenced to a 5 year to life term in state prison. The sentence was later amended to read no parole for at least 50 years.

But Violet Berling did not have to spend 50 years in jail. On March 18, 1964, she was granted parole with the stipulation she not be around small children. She changed her surname – adopting her mother's vaudeville stage name – Schauer. On December 17, 1974, while living in Anaheim, she was discharged from the criminal justice system. Violet continued to live in California, dying in Los Angeles on February 27, 1983.

Teen Murderers

Many in the 1950s believed the reason teenagers were getting out of control and turning to drugs and crime was because Communists were trying to subvert the youth of America. "They do not care so much about the adults whom they consider as already contaminated with the disease of Capitalism and consequently of little use to them," Long Beach author Fred Schwarz wrote, "but the children are different. They can do something with them." Books, music and films were the preliminary steps towards winning American youth, Schwarz believed, slowly enticing the younger generation away from parental and American social values. Others believed it was because they could not face the realities of the atomic age, the uncertain world they were living in was too much for them and they were seeking to escape from reality by using alcohol and drugs.

Was this happening in Long Beach, which had always been such a pleasant place to raise a family? Perhaps, as a series of articles in the *Independent* in January 1950 pointed out. A former marijuana user gave the press the story:

Right now, in Long Beach, it's nearly as easy for any kid to buy marijuana as it is for him to get chewing gum. All he's got to do is know the "right people." Those "right people" are a gang of local youths who loaf around street corners downtown. They don't work or go to school, but they smoke marijuana. A few are real "heads" – they use heroin and morphine. Most of these "right people" know a lot of other kids who go to high school or college. They want their

*school buddies to smoke them, too – at four or six bits a throw.
(Independent 1/16/1950)*

It seemed the narcotic sifted down in stages from big-time wholesalers who imported their "grass" in bulk from Mexico, or else grew it themselves. They would divide it into one or two pound lots and sell it to middlemen. In turn these middlemen would break it down into "cans." A "can" was a flat tobacco tin which sold for $15. You could also buy a pound for $60. That's when the "right people" entered the scene. They would buy a can for $15 and roll it into 60 or 70 joints, sell enough joints to return their investment with a profit and still keep some to smoke themselves. Some would sell the whole works and use the cash to buy "junk" – heroin or morphine.

The State of California in 1950 had this to say about marijuana:

*Marijuana is considered one of the most dangerous drugs known.
It directly attacks the nerve centers of the brain and violently affects
the mentality and the senses. In almost every case, it causes a gradual
collapse of morals. Natural inclinations become abnormal desires,
and lead to the most revolting crimes. Marijuana is the direct cause
of such crimes. (Independent 1/16/1950)*

The article went on to describe a 17-year-old Long Beach girl from a good family who was introduced to marijuana. After smoking it for three months she found out she was pregnant. She couldn't even remember who the father might have been. Another 15-year-old boy held up a gas station with a stolen revolver to support his marijuana habit.

Many marijuana smoking youths formed "wolf pack gangs." They would pile into their hot rods and prowl the streets at night looking for a fight. When they found a likely victim they took turns beating the innocent prey.

Though this 1950 newspaper depiction of marijuana may seem a bit over dramatic when viewed from the present day, by May 1950 several people had been attacked by gangs and seriously injured; one had even been murdered.

On May 27, 1950, three members of a teenage "crime club," two of them girls, were booked in connection with the robbery-slaying of Dominic "Mickey" Calarco, who owned a liquor store at 742 E. Seventh Street in Long Beach. Seventeen-year-old Thomas Charles Cook admitted firing the fatal shot. Tommy Cook, who turned 18 after the crime, was deemed an adult in the eyes of the law and ordered to stand trial for murder. His accomplices included Muriel Clare (aka Pickles) Downs, also 17, who took her father's gun to use in a May 12th robbery, and 15-year-old Peggy Brynes.

Brynes, an avid reader of true crime stories, used the ideas she obtained from crime magazines to stage real ones, according to the press. She took notes on what she read, critiquing the fictional scenarios and planning ways to make their real life counterparts more successful. She even got the rest of the gang involved, having them come up with a name for each intended crime, just like a book title. After much thought she even came up with a name for the gang – Cherokee Raiders.

It was Peggy who "canvassed" the liquor store, going in and buying some Cokes. When she came out she told the other two where the cash register was and how many customers were in the store. Then Muriel, dressed in jeans to look like a boy, and Tommy went in and looked at some magazines and waited until a customer left. Peggy acted as lookout and driver of the get-away car.

With no one else in the store to possibly identify them, Tommy and Muriel staged the holdup. The young veteran manning the store, 26-year-old Dominic Calarco, pleaded for his life, telling the teens he had a wife and two kids.

At his trial, Tommy Cook admitted he softened and told Calarco to keep the money. Tommy stated he started to back away and began to put the gun in the holster when Calarco reached over the counter and swung at him. Tommy then redrew the gun and backed away, but Calarco said to wait and he'd give him $5. When Calarco stepped toward Cook, Cook claimed he panicked. He fired a warning shot at the veteran and turned and fled. But Calarco's supposed fear had just been a pretense to put Cook off guard. Calarco rushed Cook, overtaking him in the middle of Olive, just south of Seventh Street. During the struggle Cook fired one shot, severing Calarco's jugular vein. Calarco died shortly after at St. Mary's Hospital.

Witnesses told another story. A sailor testified he was driving by the liquor store when the fatal shooting occurred. He saw Calarco throw bottles at the fleeing youth and saw the teenager fire four or five shots while running. Cook slipped and partially fell to the pavement as Calarco caught him. As Cook rose from the ground he fired another shot killing Calarco. Marjean Handley, a Douglas Aircraft worker, told the court she saw Tommy running out of the store with Calarco behind him. Calarco caught him and they struggled. She heard Tommy telling Calarco to give him the money, but Calarco refused. Then four or five shots were fired and she saw Calarco drop to the pavement.

Tommy Cook and the two girls fled the scene. At school the next week they decided to recruit other members for the gang, Larry H. Collins, 14, and Shirley Jean Armitage, 16. Two weeks after Calarco was killed they robbed a Compton liquor store. Collins was captured and the other gang members later traced.

Tommy said they did the robberies because Peggy was pregnant and they had to get hold of some money. They decided to enlist Muriel since she had a gun. The trio later admitted they were "stupid" for doing it, though they showed little sign of remorse, according to the press. Their biggest fear was facing up to their parents.

Albert Ramsey, superintendent of the Navy Chapel of Grace Sunday School, was also an attorney. He had known Tommy Cook from Sunday school days and agreed to act as his lawyer. Issues brought out at the trial included the fact that Peggy and Tommy considered themselves married and she believed she was pregnant. Ramsey referred to the teenagers as "children" or "youngsters" throughout the trial. He pictured Cook as a young child who had never known his father and who had been shoved from foster parent to foster parent, never sure of shelter or food and working when he could for the necessities of life. He said the youngsters lived in a confused, make-believe and complex world – a world of crime comic books, sex magazines and gangster and western movies. Ramsey contended Cook abandoned the attempted robbery of Calarco's liquor store and was "running for dear life" when tackled by Calarco. Pointing to the evidence which asserted several shots were fired before Calarco was killed; Ramsey claimed Cook, a sharpshooter, couldn't have missed the 202-pound Calarco at such close range unless he intended to do so. Therefore, Ramsey told the jury, Cook couldn't be guilty of first or second degree murder but should be punished for the armed robbery and attempted armed robbery.

The prosecutor in the case, Thomas Cochran, called Cook and the girls a "gang" and a desire for excitement was the motivation.

On September 1, 1950, Tommy Cook was found guilty of murder in the second degree by a jury of eleven women, and one man. He was sentenced to serve a five-years-to-live term on the second-degree murder charge and another five-years-to-life term for the armed robbery of the Compton liquor store. On the charge of attempting to rob the Calarco store, Cook received a 2 to 20 year sentence to run consecutively. Both underage girls were sent to the Ventura School for Girls run by the California Youth Authority (CYA).

Despite shrieks from Dominic Calarco's mother-in-law shouting that Tommy should have gotten murder in the first degree, Attorney Ramsey pleaded with the court to also commit Cook to the Youth Authority. He portrayed the young slayer as a child from a broken home who had never known anything but a life of insecurity. For all but two weeks in his life, when he was involved in the gang, Ramsey argued, Tommy had lived an exemplary life. The court, however, felt differently. Thomas Cook, now 18, was sentenced to serve his time in San Quentin prison.

Because of Ramsey's efforts Tommy got a break and was sent to Soledad Prison instead of San Quentin. He started studying for his high school diploma. In 1956, Tommy was paroled. He said he planned to become a salesman, would not return to Long Beach, but would remain within the state. On May 26, 1961, he was released from parole – now a free man.

Lawrence (Larry) Horace Collins was just 14-years-old when he was arrested with Cook while attempting to rob a Compton liquor store. Not involved in Calarco's murder, he was tried as a juvenile and sentenced to a California Youth Authority institution. He continued to run into trouble with the law. In 1952, he was sent again to a CYA institution for possessing marijuana. In 1956, federal authorities caught him trying to smuggle heroin into the United States from Mexico. He was treated for narcotic addiction. In June 1958, he returned to Long Beach and in September was arrested for possessing and selling drugs. While in the city jail he tried to commit suicide. He tightened one end of a belt around his neck, wrapped the other end around the rung of a top bunk and jumped. Other prisoners loosened the belt and called for help. Collins was taken to Seaside Hospital where it was thought his neck had been broken, but X-rays revealed no fractures. He returned to his cell, wearing a neck brace. He was later transferred to county jail where he became an "informer."

His parole officer told probation investigators that the government needed to take exceptional care of Collins to prevent him from being reached by persons who might harm him. Two attempts on his life were made before he was granted a single cell. Collins was later sentenced to serve 10 months for violating parole on another narcotics offense.

Carmella Calarco kept her husband's liquor store at 742 East Seventh Street. However she found it difficult to care for the children and the store simultaneously. She arranged for her four-year-old son to live with his maternal grandmother in San Diego, but kept her eleven-month-old daughter with her. She said it was a challenge changing diapers between customers, but as Maria got older she was able to send her daughter to a private school during the day. After the trial Carmella received a few unpleasant telephone calls, some of them leaving her in tears. They were mostly from people who criticized her and her dead husband for being in the liquor business. One caller expressed satisfaction that Mickey Calarco had been killed. Reporter Malcolm Epley said Mrs. Calarco just wanted to forget the killing and get on with her life.

Could a baby sitter go berserk and end up killing the child she was watching? Could viewing a television program have caused a teen to blur the distinction between fiction and reality? The answer to both questions appears to be "yes;" it happened on December 29, 1951. On that Sunday evening 16-year-old baby sitter, Delora Mae Campbell, strangled her 6-year-old charge, Donna Joyce Isbell, with a sock. Why had she done such a thing? Delora told authorities an incoherent story of watching a television drama called "Repeat Performance" and then having a "vision" of Donna Joyce "dead with a green necktie around her throat."

The television thriller featured a woman who had shot her husband given a year to relive her life prior to the shooting in a manner leading to a different solution. Delora, a Woodrow Wilson High School sophomore, told authorities she watched the television program while babysitting for the Isbell family at 2913 Nipomo Street in Lakewood Plaza. After viewing the thriller Delora put Donna to bed about 10 p.m., and then she and 8-year-old Roy Jr. watched a western movie until she tucked Roy into bed alongside Donna.

After doing the dishes Delora started seeing "visions" of Donna with a red and green necktie around her neck. Delora searched the house for such a neckpiece but couldn't find one. She then took a sock belonging to Roy Isbell Sr. and tied it tightly around the neck of the sleeping 6-year-old. Delora gave it a hard pull and stuffed part of a bedsheet into the child's mouth to prevent her from crying out. Donna Joyce then raised her arms once and then dropped them, the teenager told police.

At this point Delora seemed to come out of the trance which had mesmerized her since watching the television drama. She realized what she had done. She ran out of the home and aroused neighbors, Doctor and Mrs. Willner. Delora told them of her "dream" and asked the doctor to come with her to the Isbell home to see if the dream was true. Puzzled, Dr. Willner accompanied the girl and found the body of the child. He then called police a few seconds before Garnette Isbell, a swing shift worker at Douglas Aircraft Company, arrived home. The father, a chief petty officer at Los Alamitos Naval Air Station was on 24-hour duty at the time of the tragedy.

Delora had been baby-sitting for the Isbell's for 6 weeks – on the nights Roy Isbell had all-night duty at the air station. Delora arrived at the household about 3 p.m. and stayed until Garnette Isbell came home at 1 a.m. Delora, who lived with her aunt and uncle a few blocks from the Isbell home came to her relatives' home three months earlier after running away from her parent's home at Ft. Lupton, Colorado. She ran away, she stated, because she hated her brothers and sister and wanted to strangle them.

A Colorado court ordered her committed to the Colorado State Industrial School, but she was placed on two years of probation after her aunt, Lavada Regan, offered to take her in. The Regans said she was a model young girl and an excellent student. They were surprised however to learn of Delora's addiction to murder mysteries – in books and on television.

Delora told authorities she killed Donna, but didn't have any reason, except having a vision of Donna with a necktie about her throat. She said she had similar "visions" in which she saw her eleven-year-old brother, Dickie, strangled with a necktie around his neck, but never had acted against him. A compact found in Delora's cell added to the bizarre nature of the case. Delora had scratched words on the compact with a bobby pin the first night she was in jail. It read "Delora Mae Campbell killed Donna Joyce Isbell Saturday night, Dec. 29, 1951."

Donna Joyce Isbell was buried January 2, 1952, in Forest Lawn/Sunnyside Memorial Park. The doll she wanted so badly for Christmas, but hadn't received, was buried with her. She had told her parents she wanted a talking-walking doll, but the Isbell's had decided holding off on purchasing the expensive doll until Donna's birthday on February 18th. On reading about the tragedy and Donna Joyce's desire for the doll, newlyweds Paula and William Thornton offered the Isbell's a doll identical to the one Donna wanted. The Isbell's, overwhelmed by the Thornton's generosity, accepted, and buried their daughter with it. The doll manufacturers later gave Paula Thornton, 17, a new doll.

There was much discussion following the Isabell murder about the subliminal effect television and movies could have on the mind. Could the veil between reality and fiction become confused, resulting in a reenactment of the fictional drama by a susceptible individual? It was a debate that would go on for years.

Delora was sent to Camarillo State Mental Hospital in April 1952. During her stay at Camarillo Delora's mental condition improved and, as a result, she was allowed freedom of the institution's grounds. In April 1954, she simply walked away. Hospital authorities assured the public the girl was not dangerous. She had saved $70 while at Camarillo – money she earned for doing work at the hospital – and had taken a bus to Bakersfield. She later returned to the Long Beach area and contacted her aunt and uncle, Mr. and Mrs. Gene Regan, who helped police in apprehending her.

How long Delora remained at Camarillo, or if she is still there, is considered "confidential" information. It can only be released 75 years after the patient's death, or release.

On November 10, 1957, as Lela Mae and Harold Miller were taking their 15-year-old son Larry back to the Fred C. Nelles School for Boys, a detention home in Whittier, after a Sunday afternoon outing, the Long Beach youth ran away. The boy, serving time for car theft, soon became the prime suspect in the sex murder of 22-month-old Laura Helen Wetzel of Rolling Hills Estates.

Mrs. Wetzel was searching the neighborhood for her child, who had slipped out of her home unnoticed, and had gone next-door to the Stafford Thurmond home to see if they had seen Laura. When they didn't respond to her knock, she tried the door and found it unlocked. Thinking they just couldn't hear her, she ventured inside only to discover John Laurence (Larry) Miller in the Thurmond home. Another neighbor, Francis King, heard Mrs. Wetzel scream that there was a man in the house with a knife and gun.

As King ran up to investigate he was confronted by Miller who pointed a .22 automatic pistol at him. Miller told King if he came in the house he would kill him. King tried to calm the teen down, saying they simply were looking for a lost baby and had the boy seen the child. Looking confused Miller slammed the door in King's face. An alarmed King returned to the Wetzel's house and called police. As Mrs. Wetzel and the Kings watched the house the police arrived, but the youth had already slipped out the back door. Later, Laura's nude, bruised, lifeless body was found by her mother under a bed in the Thurmond home. The coroner's report indicated the child had been smothered and molested. Miller was identified by fingerprints found at the scene and from a picture seen by Mrs. Wetzel.

Stealing a car and robbing a grocery store, Larry Miller headed into Oregon and later Nevada. He was captured in Reno, Nevada, on November 15th. He might have gotten away but he made one mistake: he picked up a hitchhiker who later alerted police.

Miller admitted to strangling the girl. He was going to cut her up, but got the willies. He told authorities he went to the Thurmond home because he knew them. He wanted to steal a gun from their gun collection. Laura was out front when Miller called her into the house. He declared he wanted to kill somebody and she was around so he put his hand over her mouth and nose and suffocated her. He waited for the Thurmonds to come home. His plan was to club Mr. Thurmond and force Mrs. Thurmond, under knifepoint, to take him to a bank and withdraw money. He was then going to tie them up, take their car, drive to the airport and get away. While he was waiting for the Thurmonds, Mrs. Wetzel came looking for her child. When Miller threatened her with a knife she ran out and called a neighbor.

Knowing they would call the police he stole a bike and then a car and took off.

On December 27, 1957, John Laurence Miller sat impassively as he heard himself alternately described as "the most vicious, treacherous and cold-blooded murderer in Long Beach area history," and "a sick boy." Psychiatric reports showed the youth had superior intelligence but was a person devoid of any feeling. Young Miller said he'd been close to killing before and just decided he might as well get it over with. He said he'd been thinking of killing his father since he was 7-years-old, but didn't because there'd be no money coming in if he did. Psychiatrists said the youth had a deep-seated hatred of his father and suggested Laura Wetzel served as a substitute in the young man's mind for the father he really wanted to murder.

Because of his age, Miller could not be executed. Instead he was sentenced to life imprisonment for the murder of Laura Wetzel. He swore vengeance on his captors and boasted that his prison stay would be a short one. His parents sat in the rear row of the courtroom. The youth neither said hello nor goodbye to them. They left immediately after the sentencing. Few realized that Deputy Long Beach District Attorney Ted Sten's statement that Miller would "kill again before he's through," would come true.

In August 1975, 33-year-old Larry Miller was released from the men's prison at San Luis Obispo after serving nearly 17 years for the murder of Laura Helen Wetzel. He returned to his parent's home, and after a family quarrel his parents threw him out. Even though they clashed, they did care enough to pay for a room for him in a downtown Long Beach hotel. This was to be their last compassionate act. On October 21, 1975, Lela Mae and Harold Miller, 5450 Flagstone Street, were shot to death by their son.

Harold Miller managed to stagger to the home of a neighbor before collapsing. Lela Miller was found wrapped in a blanket in the blood stained bedroom of the couple's home. Several empty .25 caliber shell casings were found in the home, and a large mirror had

126

been shattered by a bullet. Police also found blood smeared on the front door knob which had dripped around the entrance.

It appeared Larry Miller had shot his mother after an argument, dragged her body into a bedroom, and then waited for his father. When Harold Miller appeared he shot him too. Larry Miller managed to evade police for a week after the killings of his parents, but was arrested on October 28th trying to hold up a Bank of America in Downey.

During the robbery Miller pulled a gun from his waistband, told the bank manager he was "a parolee with nothing to lose," showed him a newspaper clipping describing the grisly murder of his parents and demanded money. As the bank manager, Marshall Alfson, collected money from the tellers he whispered to one to push the alarm for the police. The teller did, and Alfson continued calmly to collect the cash on hand. When through, he handed the $1,841 to Miller. Miller then demanded that Alfson accompany him out the door. The police were waiting. Miller was arrested, offering no resistance.

Following a five-day trial Miller, acting as his own attorney, urged jurors to find him eligible for the death penalty. On April 19, 1976, John Laurence Miller was sentenced to die in the state's gas chamber, which at that point hadn't been used since 1967. He greeted the sentence with approval saying he would abandon the appeal of his conviction that was automatic under state law.

In January 1977, Miller added fuel to his death sentence by admitting to killing Donald A. Diller and leaving him in a La Mesa motel room October 8, 1975. Diller, a musician, had been shot in the head. Why had Miller now confessed? He just wanted to brag about another of his "accomplishments."

Was Larry Miller a psychopath? He definitely exhibited callousness, lack of empathy, overconfidence, selfishness and violence, all signs of a psychopathic personality. Was he born that way or was it something he experienced in his youth, perhaps abuse from his father, which brought on criminal tendencies at an early age?

At the time of Miller's conviction in 1976, the death penalty was a political hot potato in California. It wasn't until April 21, 1992, after years of debate, that Robert Alton Harris became the first person executed since 1967. As of this writing (June 2018) John Laurence Miller remains in prison in Lancaster, California. Laura's mother's wish seems to have come true. Upon his capture she told the press "I hope he's locked up forever and ever so he won't hurt anybody else.

Hot rods were a national passion, certainly among 1950s and 60s teenagers, who conferred names to their cars and related to them much more closely than teens do today. Teens back then saved their money to buy a car and then kept adding to it – this week a new radiator, next week a muffler. In the end it seemed as though the cars had been nurtured scrap by scrap into existence. One of the key components of a hot rod was a radio, where songs such as the Beach Boys' ode to cars "409" could be played. Teenagers cruised into A&W Root Beer stands where carhops served them on roller skates. Girls dressed in bobby sox and poodle skirts, while leather seemed to appeal to young males. Adding to the culture of the day was a new type of theater perfect for the hot-rod, teen set – the Drive-In.

In Long Beach the Circle Drive-In was the place to hang out. Opening on April 4, 1951, the new theater was hailed as the most modern of its type in the nation; it also had the largest screen of any drive-in in the country measuring 70 feet by 46 feet. To make sure it remained a wholesome place to bring families, staff patrolled the parked cars looking for foggy windows and unobservable bodies, pounding on windows until couples rose for air.

This bygone era was nostalgically portrayed in the television sitcom *Happy Days* (1974-1984), but all was not as wholesome as the Fonz and Richie led viewers to believe.

There were good teens, and there were troublesome teens. It was a headache, law enforcement officers told reporter Don Neff in 1961, to tell which was which. It was especially difficult when trying to distinguish gang members from car club members. Both wore special jackets and painted names on their cars. Most car clubs had a good bunch of youngsters, sponsored by law enforcement and civic organizations, who participated in community projects.

In Long Beach the Associated Car Clubs of Long Beach, the first of its kind in the nation, was formed by nine local car groups in June 1951. Members realized they needed a responsible central organization which would have the approval of police and civic groups.

One of the necessary qualifications for membership was to pass the California Highway Patrol's test for safe vehicles. The association also sought places where members could test their cars, conduct speed and timing tests and enjoy drag racing. Officer Gordon Browning, who worked for 11 years with car clubs, estimated there were 1500 such groups in Los Angeles/Orange counties in 1961, with an average membership of 15 to 20.

But not all car clubs were "responsible" associations – some turned into gangs. Fights often ensued over the slightest issue, as 16-year-old Neil Mahan found out the evening of March 28, 1960.

It had been young Neil's dream to "belong." He desperately wanted to be part of the "in group" of car club members, many of whom identified with James Dean and Dean's 1955 film *Rebel Without a Cause*. In real life Dean was a car racing enthusiast, a trait emulated by many car club members. Dean's death in a car accident in September 1955 raised his image to cult-like status. Drag racing among the clubs "a la James Dean style" became the "in" thing to do, as did clashes between rivals.

Though he didn't own a car, the Townsmen car club allowed Neil Mahan to join the organization. Six weeks after joining the Townsmen Neil Mahan was shot and later died following a clash between the Townsmen and a rival car club, the Dutchmen.

The trouble had begun two weeks earlier when a Townsmen club member was attacked with a railroad spike. No one knew who the attackers were, however some Townsmen were sure Dutchmen car club members were responsible. The Townsmen decided to get even.

The retaliatory attack was carried out with military precision. A girlfriend of one of the Townsmen found out about a meeting the Dutchmen were holding and passed the information on. The 20 Townsmen members, whose trademarks were goatees and tall black top hats, were told to wear white T-shirts so they could identify themselves in the crowd. They armed themselves with knives, hatchets, bayonets, baseball bats and tire irons, in addition to a gun carried by the murderer.

The Townsmen rendezvoused at a drive-in and then proceeded to the Moose Lodge where the Dutchmen were holding their meeting. Surrounding the building, the Townsmen smashed windows and when entering the building wrecked games and vending machines. Three shots were fired. One hit Neil Mahan in the head. When he fell the scared invaders beat a hasty retreat. Mahan died four days later at Community Hospital from a gunshot wound in the brain.

W. L. Williford, governor of the Moose Lodge and supervisor of the Dutchmen car club, could not understand the attack. He said the Dutchmen were all good kids. Why then had they been targeted by the Townsmen?

Police weren't so sure about Williford's claim about the Dutchmen being "good kids." Police records revealed a long list of "bad blood" incidents between the Dutchmen and the Townsmen. It seemed one thing led to another, there appeared to be no end to revenge between the two groups.

The attack, and Mahan's death, had all the local car clubs talking. One Townsend want-to-be, Eddie W. Padilla, bragged that he had been the killer. When word of this was leaked to the police, Padilla changed his story. He vowed he had not purposely tried to kill anyone. He was trying to become a member of the Townsmen so went along when they raided the meeting of the Dutchmen in the Moose Lodge. He brought along a .25-caliber pistol he had purchased the previous month for "protection" after a fight with a boy who was not a member of any car association. He also admitted driving to the raid with five others who were not members of the Townsmen. When he reached the meeting place, he stayed outside and fired through a window. Then he ran.

Nineteen Townsmen club members were arrested for the violence that resulted in Mahan's death. The sponsor of the Townsmen, 30-year-old Edward Brick, was also taken into custody. He had assumed the role of sponsor so the boys could be admitted to the Associated Car Clubs of Long Beach. He said the group was hoping for a "peace talk" with the Dutchmen but things got out of hand. Upon further questioning he admitted he had encouraged members to bring weapons, in case things didn't go well. However, he denied knowing anyone had a gun.

At Brick's hearing Judge Charles T. Smith said he was "shocked to see such an organization headed by a man who did not have enough common sense to stop this thing." The judge did note that some of the young men voluntarily gave themselves up, but he believed this was because of parental pressure.

Twenty-one year old Eddie W. Padilla was convicted of manslaughter and sentenced to 1 to 10 years in prison. The other 18 Townsmen defendants – Frank Pollard, Edward Brick, Randell Check, David Hill, Mickey Mefford, Gene Stivers, James Minnis, Lawrence Wieland, Ernie Verdugo, John Pontrelli, Gilbert Valdez, Albert Valle, Charles Brown, Tom Haines, Richard Padilla, Jack Sport Armando Gonzales and James Hall – pleaded guilty to conspiracy to commit assault. Eight drew jail terms, 2 received probation and the rest were sent to the California Youth Authority. John Pontrelli and James Hall, who received probation, lost their driving rights for three months, were barred from associating with their co-defendants and were forbidden to belong to any organization except church groups without Probation Department approval.

Many hot rod car clubs had died out by the mid-1960s. By then major car manufacturers were making muscle cars for the young male market, and the car builders and racers of the 1940s and 50s had jobs and family responsibilities.

Epilogue

National crime figures released in 1957 revealed a 70% increase in juvenile court cases since 1948. It was estimated that in 1957 alone 530,000 youngsters would be called into court. Was this increase, as Long Beach's Dr. Fred Schwarz believed, a result of Communist interference into American life?

Has Communism influenced American life today? Has it infiltrated our society? Have the Russians waged a non-military war of propaganda, infiltration, subversion and demoralization? In the 1950s and 60s many believed this to be true. But as time went on, many dismissed it as a Communist scare that never quite appeared. By the 21st century such a notion seemed outdated. But after the U.S. presidential election of 2016, people are again wondering if Russia is indeed following the Communist principles outlined by Fred Schwarz and others.

In a December 1953 speech Schwarz warned members of the Long Beach Chamber of Commerce that "Communists are scientifically preparing for the execution of American families."

Was Schwarz right? Were American family values headed towards extinction? A 2014 Pew Research Center report revealed that fewer than half (46%) of American youth younger than 18 years old are living in a home with two married heterosexual parents in their first marriage. This is quite a change from 1960 when 73% of children matched this description. One of the largest shifts in family structure is that 34% of children today are living with an unmarried parent – up from just 9% in 1960. Americans are delaying marriage and many forego the institution altogether. At the same time, children born outside of marriage now stands at 41%, up from just 5% in 1960.

The so-called "baby boomer" generation (1946-1964) talked about in this book, grew up in a time of dramatic social change. Their experiences in the Cold War were very different from those of their parents. While adults perceived Communism as a threat to the American way of life – to their health and well-being and those of their families – their children learned to fear the loss of a future they could grow into and inhabit. These kids of the Atomic Age wondered if they might be the last children on Earth. They were raised on civil defense films, tales of nuclear annihilation, and a world taken over by Communism. Instead they became the wealthiest, most active, and most physically fit generation up to their era and lived to see the Soviet Union dissolve into 15 independent countries in 1991. Will they also live to see the official end of the Korean War, and the reunification of North and South Korea? Time will tell.

Bibliography

UFOs

"Airmen see quick, shiny things: flyniks clutter up southland skies." *Press-Telegram*, 6 November 1957.

Anderson, Carl. *Two Nights to Remember.* Los Angeles, New Age Publishing, 1956.

"Atomic energy now hinted as source of mystery sky discs." *Independent*, 6 July 1947.

Beckman, Bob. "Flying saucers seen 2nd time by some." *Press-Telegram*, 4 January 1961.

Beckman, Bob. "Saucer sighters 'mum' 2nd time." *Press-Telegram*, 5 January 1961.

Beckman, Bob. "Ten-year study finds no 'saucer' evidence." *Press-Telegram*, 6 January 1961.

Beckman, Bob. "UFO reports dwindle but most who reported seeing flying saucers still certain of it." *Press-Telegram*, 3 January 1961.

Bethurum, Truman. *Aboard a Flying Saucer.* Los Angeles, DeVorss, 1953.

"Captain Graves sees things: strange phenomena witnessed in the sky." *Daily Telegram*, 6 July, 1907.

Christopher, Paul. *Alien Intervention: the spiritual mission of UFOs.* Lafayette, Louisiana, Huntington House Publishers, 1998.

Cooper, Helene. "Glowing Auras and 'Black Money': The Pentagon's Mysterious U.F.O. Program." *New York Times,* 16 December 2017.

Crawford, Jamie. "NY Times: Pentagon study of UFOs revealed." *CNN*, 17 December 2017.

Dennett, Preston. "Is there an underwater UFO base off the Southern California Coast?" *FATE*, February 2006.

Dennett, Preston. *Undersea UFO base: an in-depth investigation of USOs in the Santa Catalina Channel.* Los Angeles, Blue Giant Books, 2018.

Emery, Dave. "Sizzling Stone Puzzles." *Press-Telegram,* 23 September 1954.

Eres, George. "AF members swear to seeing big saucer." *Independent*, 23 March 1950.

Fager, Jeff. *Fifty years of 60 Minutes.* New York, Simon & Schuster, 2017.

"Flying saucer data restricted." *Independent*, 8 April 1949.

"Flying saucer reported here." *Press-Telegram*, 4 May 1952.

"Flying what's it will land here at new home base this afternoon." *Press-Telegram*, 18, April, 1954.

"Glowing saucer crosses sky: four Long Beach folk see mysterious visitant." *Press-Telegram*, 30 July 1947.

Griswold, Earl. "Guard tries to gun down flying saucer, hits object." *Press-Telegram*, 18 July 1967.

Griswold, Earl. "Lakewood today." *Independent Press-Telegram*, 26 December 1957.

"Guard decides he was mistaken. Saucer shooting balloons out of proportion." *Press-Telegram*, 19 July 1967.

Hanson, Kristopher. "On the surface of it, UFOs could lurk." *Press-Telegram*, 17 January 2007.

"Here we go again, folks, more saucers!" *Independent*, 7 February 1948.

"Here's why Mon-Ka failed to show up." *Press-Telegram*, 15 November 1956.

Holly, Chris. "The case of a UFO sighting and the spaceman of Ocean Beach." *UFO and Paranormal News from Around the World*, 16 October 2009.

"Huge towers in mirage amaze visitors at beach." *Los Angeles Herald*, 5 October 1911.

Hynek, J. Allen. *The UFO experience: a scientific inquiry*. Chicago, Henry Regenery Company, 1972.

Jacobsen, Annie. *Area 51: an uncensored history of America's top secret military base*. New York, Little, Brown and Company, 2011.

"L.B. stood up by Mars envoy." *Press-Telegram*, 8 November 1956.

"L.B. sunbather reports she saw flying disc." *Independent*, 3 June 1949.

Lewis, James R. *The Encyclopedia of cults, sects, and new religions.* New York, Prometheus Books, 1998.

"Local pilot reports seeing weird, comet-like craft." *Press-Telegram*, 31 October 1949.

"Long Beach woman reports flying saucer." *Independent*, 20 March 1950.

Manzer, Tracy. "TV news station probing UFO footage." *Press-Telegram*, 17 November 2005.

"Marine fliers spot object looking like flying saucer." *Press-Telegram*, 28 September 1949.

"Mysterious light here last night believed meteor." *Press-Telegram*, 8 March 1948.

"Mystery object hangs over L.B." *Independent*, 24 July 1952.

"Photo of mystery saucer taken as more are spotted." *Press-Telegram*, 4 July 1947.

"A polka party...in space!" *The Triangle*, 19 May 2006,

Robeson, George. "A flock of UFOs." *Press-Telegram*, 27 September 1965.

Robeson, George. "UFOs don't fly, but they sweep a lot." *Press-Telegram*, 3 August 1966.

Ruppelt, Edward J. *Report on Unidentified Flying Objects.* New York, Ballantine, 1960.

"Saucers over L.B. outrace jet." *Press-Telegram*, 29 January 1953.

"Saucers seen by others over L.B. last Friday, *Press-Telegram,* 1 August 1947.

"Saucers still flying: Long Beach police get frequent phone tips." *Press-Telegram*, 9 July 1947.

Shannon, Herb. "Face saucer reality, space hiker urges." *Independent Press-Telegram*, 28 September 1954.

"Sky showers frogs at beach." *Los Angeles Times*, 3 October 1916.

Swanson, Bob. "Oddities of 1953." *Press-Telegram*, 1 January 1954.

"Talk from space ship arranged, meet told." *Press-Telegram*, 17 September 1956.

"Ten folk see strange lights in sky." *Press-Telegram*, 9 November 1956.

"Two Long Beach Air Force men observe 'saucer' near Idyllwild." *Press-Telegram*, 22 March 1950.

"UFO reports in Lakewood, Bellflower." *Press-Telegram*, 30 June 1966.

"View here of saucer." *Press-Telegram*, 2 May, 1949.

Walters, Warren. "Mon-ka comes in loud, clear, Martian warns earth!" *Press-Telegram*, 21 September 1956.

"Was it plane, rocket or meteor?" *Press-Telegram*, 7 January 1947.

Wells, Bob. "U.S. takes space-race lead – via telepathy." *Independent Press-Telegram*, 10 January, 1960.

Welsome, Eileen. "The Plutonium Files: America's secret Medical Experiments in the Cold War." *Albuquerque Tribune*, November 1993.

Whearley, Bob. "Little lady awaiting her messiah in flying saucer." *Independent Press-Telegram*, 15 December 1957.

Whearley, Bob. "Tune in Nov. 7: Mon-ka the Martian is 'sposed to talk." *Press-Telegram*, 13 September 1956.

Zinser, Ben. "Lecturer here bares new contact with spacemen." *Independent Press-Telegram*, 21 April 1957.

Spys?

"Action awaited to free pair held in China." *Press-Telegram*, 17 March 1950.

Anderson, Jack. "KGB used spy dust on U.S. 'mole.'" *Eureka Times Standard*, 18 September 1985.

"Kin, band hail Smith, Bender; crowd cheers pair's Los Alamitos arrival." *Press-Telegram*, 19 May 1950.

"Langelle tells Russ of subversion tries." *Press -Telegram*, 26 October 1959.

"Of moles and memories." *Washington Post*, 27 July 1982.

Ridder, Walter T. "Langelle guard of heads of state." *Press-Telegram*, 10 April 1960.

"Smith, Bender return, face brief delay; pair must undergo complete checkup after China ordeal." *Press-Telegram*, 16 May 1950.

Korean War

"107 draftees leave L.B. for training camp: first local group to depart since 1945 given sendoff." *Press-Telegram*, 28 September 1950.

"452nd bomb wing called to active duty." *Press-Telegram*, 30 July 1950.

"452nd bomb wing reaches 100% authorized strength." *Press-Telegram*, 9 June 1950.

"452nd wing USAFR again to be L.B. based: photo recon. Outfit given greater number." *Press-Telegram*, 26 June 1952.

Bowditch, Arthur. "GI shrunk to 50 lbs. dies with dysentery." *Press-Telegram*, 16 September 1953.

Bowditch, Arthur. "I was a human guinea pig for the Reds." *Press-Telegram*, 15 September 1953.

Bowditch, Arthur. "Miracle drug paralyzed him, scores died." *Press-Telegram*, 17 September 1953.

"FBI probes shooting of fireman by sentry." *Press-Telegram*, 19 December 1950.

Hosking, Ev. "L.B. Air Force reservists, first in Korea, recall crisis." *Press-Telegram*, 25 April 1965.

"Indignant wives of 452nd wing men meet Sunday." *Press-Telegram*, 15 June 1951.

Karns, Harry. "Wives and mothers of L.B. wing fliers protest inequities." *Press-Telegram*, 22 May 1961.

Kendall, John. "Artukovic extradited to Yugoslavia for trial." *Los Angeles Times*, 13 February 1986.

"Korea cites 452nd Bomb Wing service." *Press-Telegram*, 20 February 1952.

"L.B.'s Bomb Wing joins Korea fray: Sgt. Clifford Hubbard, on first mission, bags Red plane." *Press-Telegram*, 10 November 1950.

"L.B. Navy Shipyard, base, Supply Depot reactivated in fetes." *Press-Telegram*, 1 February 1951.

"L.B. PW hopes he earned right to be U.S. citizen." *Press-Telegram*, 21 April 1953.

"L.B. Sergeant listed among dead captives." *Press-Telegram*, 17 August 1953.

Lembke, Bud. "Artukovic awaits day in court." *Press-Telegram*, 9 February 1958.

Lembke, Bud. "Fugitive from Tito: villain or vilified?" *Independent Press-Telegram*, 14 December 1952.

"Long Beach prisoner repatriate tells of shooting four Chinese." *Press-Telegram*, 23 April 1953.

"Mothball bombers due in 2 weeks." *Independent*, 12 July 1950.

"Only lost an arm: LB Marine thinks he's lucky." *Press-Telegram*, 16 December 1950.

"Repatriated heroes of Korea enjoy Yuletide peace – at last." *Press-Telegram*, 25 December 1953.

Resnik, Bert. "Lindbergh eaglet likes L.B., dislikes interviews." *Press-Telegram*, 14 August 1953.

Rohrlich, Ted. " Artukovic, extradited as Nazi war criminal, dies." *Los Angeles Times*, 19 January 1988.

"Second L.B. Marine gives life in Korea." *Press-Telegram*, 17 August 1950.

"Second L.B. serviceman released in POW trade: foe frees J.P. Britt, 19, Marine." *Independent*, 23 April 1953.

"Security guards tightened at local Navy, air stations." *Press-Telegram*, 28 June 1950.

"Surfside man denies part in Nazi crimes." *Press-Telegram*, 6 May 1951.

Williams, Vera. "Mother had divine message." *Press-Telegram*, 23 April 1953.

Red Scare

"All Communists in L.A. County must register by Sept. 1." *Press-Telegram*, 22 August 1950.

"Anti-Communism school on KTTV." *Press-Telegram*, 28, August, 1961.

"Battling orator escapes jail but mustn't heckle." *Press-Telegram*, 15 January 1954.

Berlinski, Claire. "Spy vs. Spy." *The Weekly Standard*, 27 December 2004.

Birnie, Helen Wood. "It's not too glamorous working for Red causes." *Independent Press-Telegram*, 16 May 1954.

Birnie, Helen Wood. "Red membership light, but influence weighty." *Independent Press-Telegram*, 23 May 1954.

Birnie, Helen Wood. "The private life of a communist." *Independent Press-Telegram*, 9 May 1954.

"Body found in ocean; murder angle checked." *Press-Telegram*, 7 April 1950.

Fleming, Louis. "Anti-Red School told victory plan." *Los Angeles Times*, 2 September 1961.

Fleming, Louis. "Probe into 'muzzling' of military asked." *Los Angeles Times*, 31 August 1961.

"L.B. employees must sign loyalty oath or lose jobs." *Independent*, 4 October 1950.

"Legion raps Spit-n-Argue Club's Reds." *Independent*, 18 February 1953.

Meyers, Derek H. "Frederick Charles Schwarz." *Medical Journal of Australia*, July 2009, p. 368.

"Navy believes subs are Russ; checking possible Nazi angle." *Press-Telegram,* 4 April 1950.

"Red agents seized in L.B. harbor area." *Press-Telegram*, 12 November 1953.

"Registration of L.B. Reds proposed by City Prosecutor." *Press-Telegram*, 26 August 1950.

Schott, Fred. "U-by-the-Sea slugger convicted of battery." *Independent*, 22 December 1953.

Sellen, Robert W. "Patriotism or Paranoia?: Right-Wing Extremism in America." *The Dalhousie Review*, vol. 43, issue 3 (1963), p. 295-316.

Zinser, Ben. "Russ seize U.S. attaché from L.B., threaten kin, relative here fearful." *Independent Press-Telegram*, 18 October 1959.

Zinser, Ben. "Who's behind propaganda from Box 27103?" *Independent Press-Telegram*, 11 May 1958.

Atomic Age

"50-lb. object from jet falls on L.B. sidewalk." *Press-Telegram*, 15 November 1965.

"AEC planning atom-waste cemeteries." *Independent Press-Telegram*, 31 January 1960.

"Atom age game for kids unveiled." *Independent,* 2 December 1951.

"Atom waste due here; ban killed." *Press-Telegram*, 22 March 1960.

"Bolt from blue falls on L.B. home." *Press-Telegram*, 22 December 1965.

"Bomb shelter permit issued." *Independent*, 28 January 1951.

Brown, Lee. "Home in Long Beach shaken up by a 'thing'." *Press-Telegram*, 21 June 1965.

"Civil Defense agency urges first-aid kit in every house." *Press-Telegram*, 15 July 1951.

Crump, Spencer. "L.B. sky rains 4-foot ice bombs; cars ripped. 50 chunks pelt busy avenue." *Independent,* 5 June 1953.

"Dial watch radiation tops that of a yard." *Press-Telegram,* 31 March 1960.

Emery, Dave. "Meteorite or prank? Sizzling stone puzzles." *Press-Telegram,* 23 September 1954.

Flowers, George C. "Earth, sky rocked by explosion." *Press-Telegram,* 17 March 1953.

Geiger, Robert E. "Bomb shelter needs told by ex-director." *Press-Telegram,* 3 September 1951.

George, Stella." Hours of mock alert tick slowly." *Independent Press-Telegram,* 17 April 1955.

George, Stella. "L. B. family faces many trials in 1st day of test." *Press-Telegram,* 13 April 1955.

"Here's a mystery that no one can see through!" *Press-Telegram,* 13 May 1954.

"Here's what to do after A-bomb attack, says U.S." *Press-Telegram,* 17 March 1950.

"Here's what to do if you are near atom-bomb blast." *Press-Telegram,* 15 September 1950.

"Hoffa to build bomb shelter." *Press-Telegram,* 26 July 1953.

"Jaycee chief blasts fuss over A-waste." *Press-Telegram,* 16 January 1960.

"L.B. bomb shelter to protect records of 'dog-tag' wearer." *Independent*, 13 May 1955.

"L.B. men tell of atom flash." *Independent,* 3 February 1951.

"Long Beach area UFOs merely falling asphalt." *Press-Telegram*, 23 July 1965.

"Long Beach family to make 3-day test of survival if H-bomb falls." *Press-Telegram*, 6 April 1955.

McCauley, Jim. "A-waste firm to face court." *Press-Telegram*, 14 January 1960.

McCauley, Jim. "A-waste plant sabotaged.*" Independent Press-Telegram*, 27 March 1960.

McCauley, Jim. "Ban on license shocks A-waste man Boswell." *Press-Telegram*, 20 December 1960.

McCauley, Jim. "Coastwise license seen as safe." *Press-Telegram*, 12 May 1960.

McCauley, Jim. "Row goes on as city ends A-truck ban." *Press-Telegram*, 16 January 1960.

Neergaard, Lauran." Report: 1950s nuclear-test fallout was widespread." *Orange County Register*, 26 July 1997.

Neergaard, Lauran. "75,000 fallout cancers possible." *Orange County Register*, 2 August 1997.

Resnik, Bert. "Flying ash caught, poses puzzle." *Press-Telegram*, 25 March 1954.

"Russian space rocket dies over L.B., plunges into ocean." *Press-Telegram*, 16 February 1967.

"Try out shelter during siren test." *Independent*, 4 May 1951.

Wallace, Paul. "L.B. windshields chip into the pitty-pocky act." *Press-Telegram*, 18 April 1954.

Wells, Bob. "Natives were not friendly: West 15th Street takes very negative side in A-waste debate." *Independent Press-Telegram*, 17 January 1960.

Whearley, Bob. "Farewell, Pike relic. Bomb shelter comes down but reluctantly." *Press-Telegram*, 30 January 1958.

Rock 'n' Roll

All music artist biography by Mark Deming. "Adrian & the Sunsets." 18 January 2018. www.allmusic.com/artist/adrian-the-sunsets

Bolinger, Fred. "Riots elsewhere, but not here." *Independent Press-Telegram*, 15 July 1956.

Carlton, Mary Ellis. "Heady success for Pyramids: scalped version of Beatles rocks teen-agers." *Independent Press-Telegram*, 23 February 1964.

Chidester, Brian. *Pop Surf Culture*. Santa Monica, Santa Monica Press, 2008.

Friend, Dick. "1500 shrieking maids go 'weepy for Eepy'." *Press-Telegram*, 23 November 1956.

"Fun Day on Nu-Pike to aid cancer foe." *Independent Press-Telegram*, 26 July 1964.

Gilbert, Eugene. "What young people think: popularity of Elvis Presley takes drop." *Press-Telegram,* 21 March 1957.

"In L.B. harbor: Elvis' gift rite runs into a snag." *Press-Telegram,* 14 February 1964.

"Invasion of Beatles has U.S. girls agog." *Press-Telegram,* 8 February 1964.

"It's bongo, man – like in drums." *Independent Press-Telegram,* 21 April, 1957.

Love, Mike. *Good Vibrations: My life as a Beach Boy.* New York, Blue Rider Press, 2016.

Peters, Donna. "Aunt Dinah's Quilting Party." *Independent Press-Telegram,* 4 February 1968.

Peters, Donna. "Getting down to the real Nitty Gritty in music." *Independent Press-Telegram,* 9 April 1967.

"Presley is rebuffed again in bid to give away yacht." *Press-Telegram,* 13 February 1964.

"Presley will strum guitar on Thursday." *Press-Telegram,* 5 June 1956.

"Rock 'n' roll frenzy jiggles nation into dizzy tizzy." *Press-Telegram,* 12 July 1956.

Sutton, Charles. "Spike Jones dies; wife at bedside." *Press-Telegram,* 1 May 1965.

Sutton, Charles "Wrecker's ball beats taps for swinging La Ronde." *Independent Press-Telegram,* 1 August 1971.

Swift, Pamela. "Nitty Gritty in Moscow." *Independent Press-Telegram*, 8 May 1977.

"Teen girls mob Rolling Stones. 10 injured." *Press-Telegram*, 11 June 1965.

Thomas, Bob. "Dick Dale's on crest of surf craze." *Press-Telegram*, 10 April 1963.

Thomey, Tedd. "Skies soak opening of the Soul Club." *Press-Telegram*, 11 April, 1967.

Thomey, Tedd. "The Twist is out, dead, kaput." *Press-Telegram*, 16 May 1963.

Wallace, Paul. "Writhing singer has L.B. soxers wailing." *Independent*, 8 June 1956.

Wiener, John. *How We Forgot the Cold War*. Berkeley, University of California Press, 2012.

A Murderous Instrument

"Berling awaits sentencing." *Press-Telegram*, 29 April 1951.

Cheatham, Chuck. "Verdugo, state's no. 1 witness, proposed to Miss Berling in jail." *Independent*, 6 February 1951.

"Child witness reverses her account of Kay's injuries." *Press-Telegram*, 16 February 1951.

"Defendant pledged fame for Kay, mother testifies." *Independent*, 6 January 1951.

Golden, Hallie. "Accordions: so hot right now." *Atlantic*, 9 January 2014.

"Jurors deliberating Violet Berling fate; Sten assails defendant as 'depraved'." *Independent Press-Telegram*, 21 April 1951.

Jury hears final plea for Berling." *Press-Telegram*, 20 April 1951.

"Miss Berling relates Kay's odd actions." *Press-Telegram*, 20 March 1951.

"Miss Berling's case opens with doctor." *Press-Telegram*, 5 March 1951.

"The people, respondent, v. Violet John Berling, appellant. January 8, 1953." *California Supreme Court. 115 Cal. App. 2d 255.*

"Verdugo struck her, Violet tells jurors." *Press-Telegram*, 21 March 1951.

"Verdugo's love letters to Miss Berling bared." *Press-Telegram*, 1 February 1951.

Vernon, Terry. "Lawrence Welk wins TV poll fourth time." *Independent Press-Telegram*, 26, February 1956.

"Vi Berling's mom sent to mental ward." *Independent,* 2 May 1953.

Williams, Vera. "Berling counsel has 9-year-old witness slap him in court." *Press-Telegram*, 15 February 1951.

Williams, Vera. "Berling jury shown how Kay and others were tied to chair." *Press-Telegram*, 17 March 1951.

Williams, Vera. "Miss Berling faces Verdugo in court, blasts prosecutor." *Press-Telegram*, 27 March 1951.

Williams, Vera. "No evidence, says Berling trial counsel." *Press-Telegram*, 18 April 1951.

"Youth to reign at Grand Medal Ball." *Independent Press-Telegram*, 23 March 1958.

Teen Murderers

Altman, Brad. "Dr. Schwarz's bank roll has Red lining." *Independent*, 12 September 1976.

"Australia speaker says U.S. sole bar to Red world rule." *Independent*, 10 September 1953.

"Baby-sitter murderer faces mental exam; displays no remorse." *Independent*, 1 January, 1952.

"Conservative traits found in Anti-Reds Stanford study on Schwarz Crusade shows." *Los Angeles Times*, 5 September 1963.

"Crusaders' Anti-Red folk songs pay off." *Los Angeles Times*, 14 October 1964.

"Donna Joyce in death gets last wish – a doll." *Independent*, 2 January 1951.

"Eight draw jail terms in car club clash." *Press-Telegram*, 3 August 1960.

Epply, Malcolm. "Beach combing (interview with Mrs. Calarco)." *Press-Telegram*, 11 December 1952.

Eres, George. "15 facing club raid death trial." *Press-Telegram*, 12 April 1960.

"Fanaticism in fight against Reds assailed." *Los Angeles Times*, 21 June 1961.

"Forum told of Red plot." *Press-Telegram*, 3 December 1953.

"Juvenile delinquency increase cited by Brown." *Los Angeles Times*, 29 June 1957.

"L.H. Collins sent back to special cell." *Press-Telegram*, 18 December 1958.

Livingston, Gretchen. "Fewer than half of U.S. kids today live in a 'traditional' family." *Pew Research Center*, 22 December 2014.

Lundburg, Ed. "Association formed by 11 L.B. car clubs." *Press-Telegram*, 24 June 1951.

Maddock, Don. "19 in car-club fatal assault plead guilty: man who fires shot sentenced to prison." *Press-Telegram*, 28 June 1960.

"Man admits gang raid shooting: helped plan attack, says sponsor 30." *Press-Telegram*, 30 March 1960.

"Marijuana easy to get here if you know right people." *Independent*, 16 January 1950.

Neff, Don. "Cars give teen-age gangs range and speed in crime." *Los Angeles Times*, 5 July 1961.

Norris, Joanne. "Missing parolee charged with murder of parents." *Press-Telegram*, 24 October, 1975.

Resnik, Bert. "Car clubs vow end to gang wars here." *Press-Telegram*, 27 April 1956.

Resnik, Bert. "Clock runs slow for Tommy Cook." *Independent Press-Telegram*, 24 August 1952.

Resnik, Bert. "Gang shooting was peace try, sponsor claims." *Press-Telegram*, 31 March 1960.

"Schwarz declares Reds foment turmoil at UC." *Press-Telegram*, 17 March 1965.

Schwarz, Dr. Fred. *You can trust the communists (to do exactly as they say)*. New Jersey, Prentice-Hall, 1960.

"Slayer Bierce gets 5 years to life term." *Independent*, 29 August 1951.

Swanson, Bob. "Vision lures Lakewood girl to slay child." *Press-Telegram*, 31 December 1951.

"Three mind experts will test slayer." *Press-Telegram*, 5 January 1952.

"Tommy Cook gang grad nabbed again." *Press-Telegram*, 18 September 1958.

"Tot killer recaptured in trap set by deputies." *Independent,* 9 April 1954.

Willman, Tom. "Miller gets his wish: to die in gas chamber." *Press-Telegram*, 20 April, 1976.

"Young killer shows remorse for action." *Press-Telegram*, 21 July 1953.

"Youth in holdup killing gets 10 years to life." *Los Angeles Times*, 29 September 1950.

"Youths' car clubs promote safety. Reckless leadfoots in jalopies passe." *Press-Telegram*, 14 October 1951.

Index

A

B

V

W

About the Author

Claudine Burnett has written several books and articles on Southern California history for which she has received numerous awards. Her credentials include a B.A. in history from the University of California, Irvine; A Master's in information science from the University of California, Los Angeles; and a Master's in public administration from California State University, Long Beach.

Several of Ms. Burnett's books have been used in the production of PBS and CSPAN documentaries. She has also appeared on television and spoken on radio. Named one of the city of Long Beach's most influential people in the cultural arts by the *Long Beach Business Journal,* she has also been described by the *Long Beach Press-Telegram* as "one of this town's finest historians." Ms. Burnett's latest book is sure to live up to her reputation as "the expert on all things Long Beach."

Printed in the United States
By Bookmasters